WARRIORS IN HIDING

THE SURPRISING PEOPLE GOD CHOOSES AND USES

BY
Doug Munton

Foreword by Dr. Roy Fish

Warriors In Hiding
The Surprising People God Chooses And Uses
by Doug Munton

Printed in the United States of America

ISBN 978-1-60647-647-5

Unless otherwise indicated, Bible quotations are taken from
The Holman Christian Standard Bible. Copyright © 2004 by
Holman Bible Publishers.

www.xulonpress.com

Dedication

This book is dedicated to my professors and friends at Wheaton College and Southwestern Baptist Theological Seminary. The faculty at these two schools did much to open my eyes to what God could do through my small life.

Acknowledgements

I want to express my grateful appreciation to the following people...

To my wonderful wife and closest friend, Vickie, who makes my life fun. She proofread, suggested and occasionally cajoled. I could not have done it without you- and it wouldn't be any fun if I could.

To my growing family- Josiah and Jarrett, Emily and Jason, Drew and Rachel. Thank you for your encouragement and love. I pray you will follow the Lord all of your days.

To Dr. Roy Fish who wrote the foreword. Dr. Fish is my hero, teacher, mentor and friend. I want to be like him when I grow up.

To my great church family at First Baptist O'Fallon, IL. They have supported and prayed and loved me despite my weaknesses. I love being your pastor.

Contents

Foreword

There is always a need in the market for a book which brings encouragement to the reader. *Warriors in Hiding* is a book saturated with encouragement.

This book is basically built around the victorious life and ministry of Gideon in the Bible and his exploits as found in the book of Judges. The more encouraging aspect lies in the fact that Gideon, at the outset, considered himself a loser with virtually no ability to be a victorious leader. Through God's supernatural help, he becomes one of the great "hidden heroes" of the Bible.

The "hidden" aspect in the title is seen in the three major parts of the book's outline. First of all, God chooses the *surprising*. Then he stretches the chosen in surprising ways. Third, God allows surprising choices.

Doug Munton, not only a very successful pastor but a competent author, spices his writing with extremely appropriate humor. Doug permits enough of himself to be seen in the book that one feels like he knows the author.

This is a book which should be ready by anyone who needs a lift along the way. It will prove to be a real tonic for the soul.

Roy J. Fish
Distinguished Professor of Evangelism Emeritus
Southwestern Baptist Theological Seminary

Part One: God Chooses Surprising People

My first sermon was quite an adventure.

After I told my family and friends that I believed God was calling me to preach, my father decided I needed to gain some experience. My father had been a pastor and knew the benefit that experience brings. So he found a very, very small church far, far out in the country (my dad was clever that way) which would allow me to preach a weekend "revival meeting".

My first real preaching experience was to be that Friday night at the small country church. I studied and prepared as best I could and showed up Friday night ready to call the masses to repentance. Only the masses didn't show up. The buses that always used to show up for the Billy Graham revival meetings never made it that night. And just before the message was to begin I knew there was a *terrible* problem.

Now I didn't know much about preaching then (some might question my use of the past tense here!) but I knew one thing. Every preacher needs to make eye contact with the congregation. As I looked out at that Friday night congregation I knew eye contact was going to be a problem.

Who could I make eye contact with? There were only nine people in the audience that night! And of those nine people, two were my parents. I couldn't make eye contact with my parents. I lived at home and still got grounded when I misbehaved. I couldn't look at them. Besides, my mother often cries when she hears me preach. There are two possible reasons why she does that. I've never had the courage to ask her which it is.

That left seven people for me to make eye contact with. And of those seven, three were my brothers! My brothers and I had many fights growing up. They knew me well. A little too well for me to preach to if you understand! There was no way I could make eye contact with my brothers.

That left four people for me to make eye contact with. And one of them was my girlfriend, who later became my fiancé, and then my wife and now is the mother of our four children! I couldn't look at her while I preached. Every time I saw her beautiful face the blood rushed to my head, my face grew red and my jaw went slack. I might have fainted had I looked her way.

That left three people for me to make eye contact with. There were two women sitting together and one of them was very, very old. I don't mean to be disrespectful, but she was exceptionally old. To my mind, she was one of the oldest women I had ever seen. There was some talk that she had dated George Washington back in the day. I mean *very* old! And the other woman was her *mother*! I wanted to make eye contact with them but they dozed during much of the message.

That left one other person for me to make eye contact with. My youngest brother had brought a friend with him that evening. (At least he *was* a friend until my brother brought him that evening.) He was a young man named Jimmy. You talk about eye contact. Poor Jimmy got a lot of eye contact from me that evening!

I thought God had made a mistake for sure. But to my surprise God was able to use a simple tool like me for his glory. And maybe just as shocking is this: God can use someone like you in some ministry as well!

It might surprise you to realize that God in heaven wants to use you to impact the world. You may not be famous or unusually gifted. Perhaps there are others who seem more capable. But God often uses the most surprising people to do his greatest works.

"What about my failures, my insecurities or inabilities?" you may ask. God often uses people who have failed. He uses the weak, the poor, the humble and the unexpected.

The poor guy never had much of a chance to be a leader. He grew up in a poor family. His mother passed away before his tenth birthday. His formal education was very limited. From an early age he had to work to support himself and his family.

Things didn't get much better as he got older. Business failure and financial setbacks plagued him. His heart was broken when his love interest rejected his proposal of marriage.

Finding some success in the field of law, he attempted to succeed in the world of politics. But a long string of painful defeats followed. He was unsuccessful in efforts to be elected to the Senate and in a vice-presidential try. He was well-acquainted with failure.

And yet, at one of the most critical junctures in American history, Abraham Lincoln stood tall. Elected president of a fractured Union, Lincoln's leadership was critical in those dark days of animosity and war. His leadership was instrumental in the abolition of the tyrannical system of slavery on American soil and in the enduring cohesion of the nation. America needed a leader and he came in a most surprising form.

You might never be called to be a politician, a pastor or to speak in front of people, but God will call you to ministry if you follow him. And often he calls the most surprising people to do some of the most surprising things.

Think of some of the surprising people God used in Bible days. David was a shepherd boy living out in the fields. His work was far from the palaces and cities. No one saw potential royalty in such a lad. When Samuel was sent by God to anoint a new king among the sons of Jesse no one thought to invite David. His own father didn't even present him to Samuel to be vetted. He was too young, too small, too unlikely. He didn't look the part of a king. But God saw his heart and made him a king.

Who would pick a fellow like Paul to be a missionary and church planter? His background was a little rough for that line of work. (Imprisoning and torturing Christians looks bad on the ministry resume, generally speaking.) Spiritually he was an enemy to the faith. The brethren back in Jerusalem had their doubts about such a character. But God saw his passion and made him an apostle.

But I don't know if there is a more shocking leader in the entire Bible than a man named Gideon. He seemed the most unlikely leader of a great uprising to free the Israelites from oppression. No one was more shocked than Gideon that God would choose to use him. But that is exactly what God did.

Gideon was hiding in a wine vat when God called him. He and others might have defined his life by his fears and his failures. But God saw what Gideon didn't see. Gideon saw a weakling but God saw a warrior.

Perhaps you have some question that God would use you in any great ways for his kingdom work. Maybe you have seen the weakness in your life. Your past may not be pleasant. Pride and doubt alternate prominence in your heart. You have failed before. Insecurities tug at your psyche. God would never use someone like you. Or would he? God has some ministry surprises for those who follow him; none greater than the kind of people God uses.

Chapter One: God Uses the Confrontational

One of my greatest surprises is that God will use confrontational people. I don't always like them. Confronters can be a little annoying and, well, sometimes downright obnoxious. They don't always know when to quit. They step on our toes and bruise our egos. But they can also be very necessary.

Jesus was willing to confront when it was needed. He called the scribes and Pharisees hypocrites and snakes and that probably hurt their feelings (Mt. 23:13-36). He turned over the tables of the money changers in the temple and that might have damaged their self-esteem (Mk. 11:15-18). While Jesus was loving and kind, he was also willing to confront when that was called for. In fact, I would suggest that Jesus was willing to confront *because* he was loving and kind.

I guess it got my righteous indignation up. I'm not normally the confrontational sort. I like to see serenity, peace and tranquility. I'm more likely to reason than rant. In-your-face is not my usual style. But this situation had me upset.

A young wife came to me deeply distraught. Her husband- we will call him Bill- had just left her for another woman. He informed her that he no longer wanted to be married and had found a new "girlfriend". So, he left his home, his wife and their baby and moved in with the other woman.

Now, this disturbed me. The husband was a new Christian. I had helped lead him to Christ and had tried to help him to grow in his faith. He was baptized in our congregation and publicly committed his life to Jesus. And now he decided to leave his family and "shack up" with another woman. Seeing his weeping wife only added to my distress. So, I decided to try some tough love.

"Do you know where Bill is right now?" I asked his wife. "Sure," she said, "he is at his new girlfriend's house." "Do you have that phone number?" I asked. "I think so," she responded. As she searched for the number I prayed for wisdom. When she returned with the number I made the call.

A female voice answered the phone. I asked, "Is Bill there?" "Yes." "Could I speak to him, please?" "Uh. . ., okay, I guess." When Bill came to the phone I said, "Bill, this is your pastor." That might have been the most awkward moment of Bill's life. When your pastor calls you at the home of the woman you are committing adultery with- well, that must be pretty near the top of the list of awkward moments!

"Bill," I said, "what are you doing?" His response was a nervous stammer. "Bill," I said, "I want you to go back to your wife and your baby and your home and quit shaming the name of Christ!" And that is exactly what he did! He repented of his actions and he and his wife then began the long, difficult task of restoring their marriage.

Sometimes God calls us to confrontation. Not every situation calls for confrontation. Often, compassion and understanding are needed. A listening and sympathetic ear is frequently the remedy. But the true nature of sin must be confronted with the truth of God's word.

May I add a word of caution about confrontation? Some of you love confrontation. You enjoy telling people what they are doing wrong. Perhaps you enjoy it a little too much. My caution to you is to pick your battles carefully. Not every issue is life or death. Not all battles must be fought by you. Not every hill is one on which you should be willing to die.

Beware of spiritual bullying. The Pharisees, remember, were willing to confront. Their problem was a lack of compassion. Confronting is not a goal to prove our zeal. It is an outgrowth of our love and a desire to point people in the right direction. Confrontation without love can be ugly and mean-spirited.

Confront when God leads and when situations require it. But don't confront for the sake of confronting. Don't fight just because it is good exercise. And, once in a while, leave a little work for the Holy Spirit. But, when God calls us to confrontation, let's not shy away because it is difficult.

We are introduced to an unusual character in the sixth chapter of Judges. God sent a prophet to confront the people with their wrongs. Prophets can be scary guys. They tend to be direct, confrontational, in-your-face. They don't seem to mind hurting our feelings or bruising our psyches. They show us the truth and tell us to get right.

When I think of prophets I think of Elijah calling down fire from heaven to consume the sacrifice. The people rallied to God and the false prophets were put to death. (I Kings 18) That's the kind of story that gets your attention!

When I think of prophets I think of Elisha who called down judgment on a bunch of hooligans who made fun of his bald head. (II Kings 2) As my hairline recedes and my remaining hair thins I like that story more and more! Balding men of the world- unite!

Prophets tend to be aggressive and direct. And God is able to use people who are willing to do the difficult, but necessary jobs. There are some moments in life that call for straight talk and direct action.

The sixth chapter of Judges tells us of a prophet like that. He spoke for God at a critical moment in the history of Israel. This passage reminds us of three things about prophets.

Prophets are Timely

Timing is everything. My oldest son, Josiah, plays the drums and is pretty good at it. When he is playing he is a whirling dervish of boom, bangs and crashes. It sounds neat and looks easy enough. On occasion, when no one else is home and the neighbors are still awake, I've taken a turn on his drum set. I bang around and mash the petals and try to whirl the drum sticks, but it just isn't the same. I don't have much of a knack for rhythm or the necessary coordination to master the timing. And what does it mean, I wonder, when all the neighborhood dogs begin to howl?

Drummers and prophets need timing. Sometimes a prophet's message is simply ignored until conditions are right and hearts are open. Sometimes the right word is just looking for the right moment.

Seven years of misery was all Israel could take. For seven long years the Midianites had ruled Israel. Judges 6 records the story of how the Midianites and Amalekites and others stole the Israelites crops and livestock. Israelites lived in fear and poverty. Verse 2 tells us the Midianites, "oppressed Israel. Because of Midian, the Israelites make hiding places for themselves in the mountains, caves, and strongholds."

Years of cave life wear on folks. People can get kind of desperate after several years of hanging around caves. Mountains, caves and strongholds are cold and dark and far from convenient shopping. The mold and mildew count *has* to be high. Bats are always hanging around and swooping in and out. You probably wake up mornings with spiders crawling through your hair. And the smell? I don't even want to think about that.

Sometimes, cave life can get bad enough to cause people to cry out to God for help. It took a while, but finally the Israelites went to God for assistance. They were tired of the humiliation and tension. Lack of food and lack of security took their toll. And, after seven years of suffering, the Israelites finally called out to the Lord.

The prophet came at a timely moment. Finally, the people were ready to listen to the truth. They were ready to consider God's answers at last.

How did God answer the great need of Israel? He sent leaders. First a prophet and then a warrior.

Does it seem odd to you that God sent leaders? He didn't have to send people, you know. He could do all that needs to be done without the assistance of anyone else. God could speak directly to people. He could write the message in the clouds. He could do the work without the aid of anyone else. God doesn't need to use people. But God wants to use people.

At just the right time God sent a prophet. Finally, the people had grown tired of the consequences of wrong choices and were willing to turn to God. Some people have to hit the rock bottom before they will look up. And when the Israelites finally called out to God he sent his prophet.

Prophets aren't the only ones God uses to confront. Perhaps you are a parent with a child who is making terrible choices. You can ignore and rationalize. Or, you can do the tough thing and confront in love. Maybe your close friends are just beginning to head down a terrible path. You can hope it will go away. Or, you can lovingly confront them about the direction of their life.

Confrontation isn't always easy and it isn't always necessary. But when confrontation is needed it is irreplaceable. God often puts us in the right place at the right time so we can deliver the right message. Maybe God will place you in someone's life who is tired of living in spiritual caves and is open to God's better plan for spiritual freedom in their life.

Perhaps some of you reading this have hit bottom. You know from first-hand experience the struggles that accompany rebellion from God. Maybe your situation has gotten bad enough, the hollowness of your life empty enough, that you are ready for the truth. You may be like the prodigal son in Luke 15. You are tired of feeding pigs and you want to go home. The Bible says of the prodigal son, "when he came to his senses. . ." (Luke 15:17). Perhaps you are ready to come to your senses and return to God.

The scalpel of God's rebuke hurts, but it is wielded to heal. God will confront you with the truth, but he does so to bring you out of bondage and into freedom. God wants fellowship and intimacy with you. He is willing to show you the obstacles in your life that keep you from that closeness.

If, like the Israelites, you are tired of living in bondage, God is willing to lead you to the path of change. Hear God's rebuke and discover God's remedy.

God's call is, however, time-sensitive. The Bible says, "Look, now is the acceptable time; look, now is the day of salvation." (2 Cor. 6:2) You can only come to God in the present tense. You can only serve him in the present tense. You can only repent in the present tense. The future tense is just a hope.

Have you ever tasted spoiled milk? Ever leave the Christmas eggnog until Easter? Some things are not meant to be put off. Prophets know God's calling is right on time and our response to that call is time-limited.

Prophets are Honest

The cowering Israelites, spoken of in Judges six, finally called on God and God sent a prophet. But all the prophet did was to tell the people that their problems were their own fault. No one wants to hear that. Prophets, however, don't seem to care very much what we want to hear. They speak for God and God tells the truth and nothing but the truth.

Honest leaders tell the truth. They don't tell people what they want to hear. They don't pick and choose what suits the modern ear. The truth matters and wise leaders know there is no substitute for it.

Sometimes, when I am asked questions on the controversial subjects of life, I answer by saying, "Do you want the truth or just what currently sounds good?" I remind people that God's truth can operate contrary to what we want to hear or what matches current popular opinion. Those who speak for God must tell the truth, even when it is unpopular or out of fashion.

God called the people of Israel to repentance. He still calls his wandering children to repentance. An honest prophet told the nation of God's requirement to change their ways just as honest leaders today are faithful to call us to repentance when we stray from God. We can react to God's call for repentance in at least three ways.

Ignore your Problems

One of my friends told me of his dad's reaction to an elevated PSA count. His father, rather than getting the proper treatment, has ignored the danger. He won't talk about the subject. He tries not to think of cancer as though that might make it go away. But it won't go away without treatment. Ignoring the problem doesn't lessen it.

Many of us are like my friend's father. We ignore God's still, small voice which beckons our repentance of sin. If we drown out God's voice, we reason, perhaps He will go away. Our reaction to God's prick of our conscience is often to turn up the volume of distraction. We immerse ourselves in work or pleasure. We look for new hobbies or projects. But the sinful behavior remains and God's call to repentance does too.

This was apparently the strategy of Israel for seven years. Despite the judgment and deprivation which God inflicted upon them, they refused to acknowledge their need for change. They ignored their problems but their problems didn't disappear.

Some people ignore their problems by turning to alcohol and drugs. Some ignore them by distractions like hobbies, television and games. But ignored problems, like the forgotten cottage cheese in the back of your refrigerator, don't go away; they just linger- and go bad.

Procrastination is a form of ignoring your problems. I became somewhat of an expert in procrastinating during my early school years. I knew I had a term paper due in a couple of weeks, but that could wait. There were more important things to do in the meantime; like trying on that new lime-green leisure suit or learning to say "groovy, man, groovy"!

My academic career, however, suffered under the load of procrastination. Waiting until the last minute meant my papers were not as well researched and well formulated. Learning to work ahead made a measurable difference in the quality of my work. (And my social life improved when I stopped wearing leisure suits and saying "groovy"!)

Procrastination must be dealt with straightforwardly. It must be overcome or it will overcome you. Simply putting off the problem does not solve the problem.

Blame Your Faults on Others

Another way to deal with God's call to repentance is to blame others. The Blame Game is big these days. Why take personal responsibility when you can blame it all on your mother, or father, or your grandparents, or your crazy Uncle Zeke? Why should you be responsible when the conditions of your childhood were really to blame? You had too little or too much. Things came too early or too late. You were indulged or deprived. How can it be your responsibility when society or someone or something else is so easy to blame?

And then some ridiculous prophet comes along saying you should repent because you are responsible. That message is as outdated as the old suits hanging in your dad's closet.

We don't like to accept blame any more than the Israelites of Gideon's day. We much prefer to shift the blame, to focus the blame on someone else.

One of the benefits of having brothers is that you never need to accept blame. When, as a boy, I got in trouble for fighting with my brothers I always had a ready excuse. "It wasn't my fault", I proclaimed. "He started it!" What a convenient excuse that was. "He started it!" I needed to accept no responsibility for my actions because, well, "He started it!"

Blaming others is easy. It is convenient. And it keeps us locked into immature thinking. We can blame our own wrong behavior on the people who "started it" in our lives.

Eisenhower had it all wrong. He gave the orders starting the invasion of Europe on D-Day in World War II. All of his preparation and all of his training culminated in this gigantic military undertaking that would determine the freedom of Europe. Yet when the order was sent and the outcome still unknown, General Eisenhower wrote this note to be given to the press in the event of the failure of the Allied forces.

"Our landings have failed and I have withdrawn the troops. My decision to attack at this time and place was based upon the best information available. The troops, the air and the Navy did all that bravery and devotion to duty could do. If any blame or fault attaches to the attempt it is mine alone."[1]

What was he thinking? He was willing to take the blame for the failure himself. Why not blame everyone else? The weather was to blame. The Generals were to blame. The soldiers were to blame. It was an intelligence failure. Someone, anyone could share the blame. But that is not what Dwight Eisenhower was going to do. He was going to take the blame.

That attitude is out of place in our modern society. We learn to shift the blame instead of taking responsibility. Even when the blame lies squarely on our shoulders we try to place it on the shoulders of others.

Sin can never be blamed on someone else. No one else can make us sin. We can be tempted by others, discouraged by others, even misled by others. But when we sin, no one else is at fault. The longer we blame others for our sin, the more distant forgiveness and spiritual freedom remains.

Take Responsibility for your Behavior

The healthy way to deal with God's repentance call is to take personal responsibility. I'm not responsible for the wrongs of others, but I am responsible for my own choices and decisions.

I love playing basketball with Milton. For the past many years, Milton and I have played together. We've been on the same team in our church league basketball and shared many pick-up games. And we have also gotten older and older.

---

[1] Stephen E. Ambrose, Eisenhower: Soldier, General of the Army, President-Elect, 1890-1952 (New York: Simon and Schuster, 1983), 309.

Milton, like me, does not want to lose. This former college basketball player knows what he is doing on the court and he plays to win. But, as our ages continue to increase, winning does not come as easily.

So Milton has to remind me and his other teammates of our responsibility. "We need this one", he exhorts. "Pressure the ball! Suck it up! Play some defense!" he demands. The fact that Milton is taller than me, older than me and often out-hustling me only sharpens my desire to go all out.

Milton and I cannot play as well as we used to play. We are neither as fast nor as quick as the old days. But we are responsible to ourselves and our teammates for how much effort we produce. "Don't let up!" Milton implores. "Keep it up!"

We need some people like Milton in our spiritual lives. We need someone who holds us accountable and calls us to our best. We need a prophet who tells us the truth about our sins and tells us to repent.

John the Baptist was a prophet like that. His primary message was "Repent!" Upon seeing the Pharisees and Sadducees coming to where he is baptizing, he cried out, "Brood of vipers! Who warned you to flee from the coming wrath? Therefore produce fruit consistent with repentance." (Mt. 3:7-8) He didn't seem to mind telling people to take responsibility for what they were doing.

Only you, with God's help, can change your behavior. Others can encourage, others can pray, others can plead, but only you can make the changes. No one can repent for you. No one can "produce fruit consistent with repentance" for you. Take responsibility for your own actions and life and allow God to do his work in your life. But don't hide behind the masks of blaming others or ignoring your problems.

Prophets are Sometimes Unnamed

Some of God's greatest servants are anonymous to most of us. In heaven, there will undoubtedly be places of honor reserved for those little known on earth. We will meet some great prayer warrior who labored long in her prayers but was too soft-spoken to garner our attention. We will be introduced to some missionary who served faithfully in obscurity. He was not the featured speaker at our conferences but he was mighty in kingdom work.

The name of the prophet in Judges 6 is never revealed. He was obedient, faithful and bold. But, he was never famous. At least, he was never famous on earth. We are never even told his name.

Some of the greatest Christian workers I know are behind-the-scenes people. They love to serve, minister and assist but never want any credit. They don't get a lot of public attention and sometimes we forget to thank them. But they serve God faithfully with few public accolades.

Beware the danger of wanting public recognition. I know that subtle call for greater prestige. I want to be lavishly praised and told how important I am. I want to be thanked profusely for my indispensable service to humanity. But I don't think Jesus saw things quite like that. He told us to serve expecting nothing in return. (Luke 6:35)

One of the nicest things a church can do is thank those who serve. It is wonderful to thank our teachers and ministry leaders and those who devote so much time and energy. But what if no one remembers to thank you? What if no one recognizes your service? What if there are no plaques, no certificates, no pats on the back? What if you do what God wants done and no one but him knows? Would you still serve under those circumstances?

We may not know the name of the prophet in Judges six, but God does. Aren't you glad God knows your name? You are not anonymous to him. He knows who you are and what you are doing. He sees and knows your faithfulness.

When I was playing High School basketball I loved to get fouled. The reason I liked getting fouled was because that meant I might get to shoot free throws. And the reason I liked to shoot free throws was because of the cheerleaders.

In my small High School, the cheerleaders had a special cheer whenever one of our team was shooting free throws. The girls would say the name of the player shooting the free throw. They said, "Sink it Doug, sink it." They clapped their hands, stomped their feet and said your name, right out loud, in front of everyone. Getting your name said publicly by some pretty girl was about the best thing that could happen to a teenage boy. Just the idea that those girls knew my name meant something special.

The Bible tells us that God knows our name. He knows how many hairs we have on our head. (In my case, that job is starting to get easier for God!) He knows our deepest needs and longings. He knows our strengths and our weaknesses. He really *knows* us. And he is our greatest cheerleader. I can almost hear him calling out a cheer now- with your name on his lips.

Others may not know you, but God does. You might be anonymous to the crowds, but you are well-known by the Lord. Perhaps you don't hear the applause of men, but you can know the applause of heaven. And that is the applause that matters.

Chapter Two: God Uses Reluctant People

It was one of the most frightening experiences of my young life. My older brother, two years my senior, was scheduled to give the devotional message at a gathering of area church youth groups. One of the youth from the host church was traditionally chosen to lead a brief Bible study and David was the natural choice in our church. He was seventeen, committed to Christ and, most importantly, willing and able to speak in front of other people.

But just before the youth were to gather, disaster struck. My brother got sick with flu-like symptoms. He would be unable to speak to the gathering that night. My mother, knowing a devotional leader was needed, volunteered me.

I tried everything to get out of the assignment. I pleaded with my mother to get someone else; anyone else. She would not listen, insisting I was up to the task. I tried to develop flu-like symptoms of my own, but mothers can see through those tricks. In short, I was stuck.

I finally picked a few verses from the Bible (always a good start to a devotional), talked as fast as I could (less time in which to accidentally swallow my tongue) and ended as quickly as I could ("Even a fool is considered wise when he keeps silent." Proverbs 17:28).

I wish I could tell you the devotional was great, but it was fairly lousy. I wish I could tell you I did it for the right reasons, but my motivation was simply to finish without life-long humiliation. I wish I could tell you hundreds of teen-agers were saved. But there were only about twenty teenagers in attendance and most of them seemed not to care too much about what I had to say. (They did seem to have a morbid curiosity about whether my nervousness might cause me to faint or publicly regurgitate, leaving them with a story they could repeat at youth gatherings for a generation.)

I was a reluctant leader to say the least. But God still used that reluctant leadership for his glory. He may have used it to bless in some small way one of the youth in attendance that night. I know he used it to begin to prepare me for the future plans he had for me. God has used many a reluctant person to accomplish his purposes. One of the best examples of a reluctant person used by God is Gideon.

The sixth chapter of the book of Judges introduces us to the very reluctant leadership of Gideon. What an unusual, surprising hero he is! He certainly did not act like David-killing lions and challenging giants. Gideon's initial response to God's call to service was to suggest the whole thing is a bad idea.

Reluctant Leaders Hide

The setting for Gideon's first encounter with God's call is instructive. The Angel of the Lord came to speak to Gideon and found the future war hero "threshing wheat in the wine vat in order to hide it from the Midianites" (Judges 6:11).

Gideon was too fearful of the enemy to thresh the wheat in the open. He knew they might steal or destroy his crop if given the chance. So Gideon hid his work down in the wine vat hoping to avoid attention.

Now I'm not a threshing expert or anything but I know the wine vat is not the best place for threshing. Separating the wheat from the chaff requires a good breeze which blows the lighter chaff away leaving the heavier grains. Wine vats are sunken and walled and wholly inadequate for threshing-unless the thresher wishes to remain hidden.

I am convinced that some of God's greatest potential heroes are hiding. They fear drawing attention to their faith. They fear the ridicule of their peers or the possibility of failure. How many great teachers, mentors and witnesses keep their talents sheltered in wine vats for fear of the enemy? They never volunteer to teach a discipleship class or help with Bible School. They never risk sharing their faith with a co-worker or classmate. In fact, they would just as soon no one at work knows they are followers of Christ. So they hide in metaphorical wine vats safe from scrutiny.

Our children used to love to play hide-and-seek. My oldest was particularly good at it. He came up with some ingenious places to hide. He hid in the clothes hamper, in closets, behind doors. I even remember once, when he was little, he climbed up into a cabinet shelf and hid behind the laundry detergent. We eventually found him, but he had a fresh, lemony scent for days!

Many Christians play hide-and-seek with God and their local church. They hide from responsibilities and from opportunities. They have no idea what their spiritual gifts may be and take no initiative to discover them. Their talents remain undiscovered and unused. They take no risks and climb no mountains. Their spiritual life is safe but dreadfully boring.

It is no fun to play hide-and-seek with God. He always knows where you are and finds you every time! You can hide your talents from your pastor, but not from God. You can shield your giftedness from your church, but not from the piercing eyes of the Lord. You might even fool yourself into thinking that you have nothing to offer, but you never fool your heavenly Father.

Three reasons we hide instead of serve

There are fears that can keep us hiding like Gideon. These worries can keep us from service. They can keep us hidden from sight instead of boldly ministering for God's glory.

One reason we hide instead of serve is a fear of failure. Many of us "play it safe" when it comes to ministry. You can't lose if you don't compete, right? Wrong! Think how much you lose if you never participate. Not participating in ministry robs you of joy, peace, spiritual satisfaction and the lessons of perseverance. You miss out on the wonderful excitement of participating in spiritual victories. You miss out on the lessons that come with spiritual defeats.

Speaking of defeats, failure is highly underrated. There are many lessons that can be learned when we get knocked down. Humility is an example. We tend to learn humility when we fall short.

A man came up to me after one of our worship services. He was all excited about my first book, Seven Steps to Becoming a Healthy Christian Leader. He said he had been tracking the sales on the internet and was delighted to see that Amazon.com had recorded 1.9 million sales of the book. That was when I had the humbling task of informing him that the 1.9 million figure on Amazon.com was not my sales, but my *rank*! My book was ranked number 1.9 million. At least I cracked the two million best seller list on Amazon!

Maybe God wants to teach you some humility. Or maybe he wants you to learn to depend upon him more. Or perhaps your need is to see God's power. God may teach you those lessons through victories or defeats.

And remember, God promises his power when we do his will in his way. I need not worry too much about hiding for fear of failure when I consider God's provision. He is bigger than any problem I will face and any difficulty I will encounter. I find a lot of comfort in that thought.

A second reason we hide instead of serve is our fear of rejection. People often reject leadership opportunities for this very reason. It is hard to lead, they reason, if no one follows. Sharing our faith is difficult for many due to the same fear of rejection.

I remember this fear of rejection in Junior High. I worked hard not to be too different or to seem too out of touch with the latest fashions and trends. I needed the right brand name and the right style. Of course, those styles look ridiculous to us today, but at the time platform shoes were a must!

Worrying about what others think of you, however, can be terribly damaging to service. Our real concern should be what the Lord thinks about us. We should care more about how we compare to God's purposes than to man's expectations.

A third reason we hide instead of serve is our fear of responsibility. Any service to God carries some responsibilities. We are to serve with excellence, live with holiness, act with compassion, etc. Why hold ourselves up to the scrutiny that comes with responsibility?

The truth is we all have responsibilities whether we use our talents or not. We are responsible by virtue of our relationship to God. Certainly, greater ministry opportunities carry greater responsibilities. But those responsibilities are part of the joy of service. Influencing people for Christ, ministering to people searching for answers, challenging others to deepen their faith; these are all responsibilities that carry great reward.

God knows your fears just as he knew the fears of Gideon. But, despite your fears, God sends his Angel to the wine vat of your life and peers down at you. He has a job for you and he calls you to a task that is breathtaking in scope and beyond what you think are the limits of your abilities.

God sees in you what others may not. God sees in you what you might not even see about yourself. God looked at Gideon hiding in a wine vat, and saw what he could become- a great warrior and leader. God looks at you, hiding behind your fears and uncertainties, and sees what you could become- a force to impact your world.

Reluctant Leaders are Unproven

"The Lord is with you, mighty warrior." That is the greeting the Angel of the Lord extends to Gideon in the wine vat. (Judges 6:12) Mighty warrior? Gideon doesn't seem like a mighty warrior. He is scared and hiding. He's never fought a battle, much less fought mightily. The only thing he has beaten is some heads of wheat and he did that in secret! But God saw what Gideon would become.

Many people are reluctant to obey God's call to service because they have never before attempted anything great for God. They don't know if they want to get in the battle because they don't know if they will hold up.

I recently read about a famous fighting force in Civil War days called "The Iron Brigade"[2]. The story was of a regiment of men from the then frontier state of Wisconsin. Part of the Sixth Wisconsin, they fought with unusual bravery and valor earning the nickname "Iron Brigade" because they stood like iron in the face of combat. When others retreated in panic, these men stood their ground and accomplished their mission.

---

[2] See Lance J. Herdegen *The Men Stood Like Iron: How the Iron Brigade Won Its Name* (Bloomington, IN: Indiana University Press, 1997).

Why were they willing to stand when others fled? Why were they brave when others gave into fear? There were three suggested reasons for their valor.

The men of the Sixth Wisconsin were well trained. They spent much of the early days of the war in seemingly endless marches and drills. These training sessions developed the discipline and almost instinctual obedience to commands so necessary in battle. Training may seem unnecessary, but it builds our instincts to do the right thing at the very time it is most needed.

Secondly, the men of the Sixth Wisconsin were well supported. They, like most soldiers of the era, were under-equipped and often underfed. They did not always have adequate supplies and sometimes lacked enough ammunition. But they had a tremendous amount of support from each other. These "westerners" had grown up together. They dared not let each other down. They were committed to the well-being of their fellow soldiers and knew they could count on the men who surrounded them. They didn't always trust the support of the Generals and decision-makers, but they always trusted the support of each other.

Thirdly, the men of the Sixth Wisconsin were well tested. One never really knows how one will react in battle until the bullets whiz overhead (or lower!). But these well trained, well supported men were ready when the tests came. They had some early victories. They were small victories, but they were victories nonetheless. These small victories led to increased confidence and bigger victories.

When people want to get active in ministry in our church we do three things. We train them, we support them and we test them. We train people in Bible knowledge and ministry skills so they have an opportunity to be successful. We surround them with a support group of fellow workers and accountability lines. But ultimately, we must test them in the front lines of ministry service. We give them small responsibilities and see how they do. We see if their gifts and talents match their ministry responsibilities. And we give them opportunities to win small ministry victories that will lead to larger victories in the future. Some of the finest Bible teachers in our church began as occasional substitutes. They discovered abilities in those limited roles which led them to greater responsibilities and expanded opportunities.

Some of the greatest future warriors in God's army don't yet know their abilities. They have never been tested in battle. They have yet to enter the fray. But God is calling them to service.

Perhaps you are a modern day "Iron Brigade" waiting to happen. God wants to use you to conquer forces of spiritual darkness and shine a bright light of eternal hope. But, like Gideon, you are reluctant and unproven. Don't doubt God's ability to use you. Don't doubt what God can accomplish through your willing service in his army. God often uses the most surprising people to win the greatest victories.

Reluctant Leaders Question

Isn't it remarkable that God uses people who have been questioners and doubters? God wants us to reach the place where our faith is firm. But he will call us to his service even when we are questioning his ability to use us. I have read of many great Christian leaders who went through times of questioning.

Billy Graham had a period of questioning. Some had raised questions with him about the authority of scripture. He had some doubts and he struggled to rectify some issues in his mind. But out of that period of questioning came a greater depth to his faith. He came to believe even more strongly in the veracity of the Bible and his faith was deepened.[3]

---

[3] Billy Graham, "Biblical Authority in Evangelism," Christianity Today, 15 October 1956, 6-7.

Gideon's response to God's call was to question God. (Judges 6:13) "If the Lord is with us" he asks, "why has all this happened?" Gideon wonders if Israel can really count on God's presence. He continues by asking, "And where are all His wonders that our fathers told us about?" Why hasn't God done something dramatic if he is really with us, Gideon wonders.

Asking questions can be a great learning tool. I encourage my children to ask questions at school, church and home. I know that asking questions can stimulate their thinking and broaden their education.

I was something of an inquisitive boy in grade school and I'm not sure all my teachers appreciated it. But in fifth grade I was blessed with a teacher who encouraged discussion and who saw questions as opportunities instead of interruptions.

One day she was teaching on the rotation and tilt of planets. It was a very interesting discussion but I had some trouble understanding the concepts. The whole discussion of the earth rotating around the sun while the moon rotated around the earth- all with tilt and elliptical orbits- well, it took some three-dimensional thinking. I wasn't getting it down exactly and so I asked some questions. Those led to more questions. And still more questions. All of these questions were patiently answered by my teacher. Finally, I felt I understood the concept fully and we moved on.

As I sat back in my chair, satisfied at last with my understanding of orbits, I noticed a stranger in the back of the room. A man had entered the classroom during our discussion and was writing notes. Then I remembered. We had been told that classroom evaluations were being done that week and this man was obviously evaluating our teacher.

Had I damaged the teacher's evaluation by my long series of questions? Was she embarrassed because it took so long for one of her students to understand elliptical orbits and gravitational pulls? I hope not. I hope the evaluator noticed instead the teacher's patience. I hope he noted that she was willing to teach a difficult concept to a somewhat difficult little boy. I hope he appreciated that she was able to handle my questions.

God is big enough to handle our questions. He might not always answer to our satisfaction. We might have trouble understanding the incredibly deep truths of his answers. He might not fully answer our questions until heaven. But God patiently teaches us. He listened to the simple, but important questions of Gideon. He will listen patiently to the questions you have as well.

Reluctant Leaders Doubt

In Judges 6:13, Gideon says, "But now the Lord has abandoned us and handed us over to Midian." He sounds like a doubting Thomas. "I won't believe unless you show me another miracle or let me see some dramatic evidence. Where are all your wonders?"

God does not give up on doubting Thomases. He is secure enough to handle our doubts and questions. He allows us to search and discover. God does this because he wants us to reach the point of genuine faith.

Some people think God is looking for blind faith. I think God is asking us for informed faith. I can trust God's faithfulness because I have read about it in his word and experienced it in my life. It is an informed faith. The more informed I am of the teaching of his word and the more I experience his grace through obedience, the deeper my faith becomes. Doubts can even lead us to a deeper, more informed faith.

One of the great things about God is that he allows me to bring my doubts to him. He invites me to search and think and ask.

A pivotal moment in my spiritual life came out of a period of questioning and doubting. I was a freshman in college struggling to come to grips with my faith. I had trusted Christ as my Savior long years before. But, some doubts about faith began to creep in. I wondered if this was my *parents'* faith or *my* faith. "Is the Bible true", I asked? "Is there a God in heaven? Is Jesus really his son and the only way to be saved?" These questions and others were part of a serious spiritual tug-of-war.

One of my well-meaning Christian friends tried to help me by suggesting that the answers to those questions didn't really matter. "After all," he noted, "following the lifestyle laid out in the Bible is still the best way to live whether it is true or not." That may well be the case, but I am not built that way. I came to a conclusion in my soul. "If the Bible is not true," I said, "and if there is no God in heaven and Jesus is not the way to salvation, then I am not going to live as though it is true. But," I added, "if it is true; if the Bible is true and there is a God in heaven and Jesus is the only hope for salvation; well, then, I am not going to live as though it is false."

I came to believe that those things are true and I have tried to build my life upon them. That period of doubt led me to real faith. My commitment to the Lord was deeper than ever and my assurance of God's provision was magnified. Finding the answer of faith came out of my questions and doubts.

I love that we can bring our doubts to God. I love that he uses us despite our doubts and questions. And, I love that in God's timing I can begin to find the answers to some of those questions.

There was no doubt in my mind that God created the world. I knew the ideas I heard in High School biology which suggested the world happened by naturalistic explanations with no need for God required a huge leap of faith. But I am so thankful for the books like <u>Darwin on Trial</u> and <u>Wedge of Truth</u> by Philip Johnson, professor at the University of

California at Berkeley.[4] I appreciate Lee Strobel's book <u>The Case for a Creator</u>.[5] Those books and others have helped me to deal with the questions and doubts about creation and evolution. My faith in God's creative work in our world is bolstered by those who take on the hard questions of science and philosophy.

I am reminded that many of my questions and doubts come because of my own ignorance. The answers are there, I just haven't yet discovered them for myself. I need not lose my faith because I have questions that are not yet answered.

Reluctant people can be used greatly by God. But when we are reluctant we need to be reminded of two things.

<u>There is always an excuse</u>. If you are looking for a reason not to get involved in ministry I can give you one. I think I have heard just about all of them! My favorite excuse came from a teenager who had to miss a ministry event because he needed to "de-thatch the lawn". (I didn't realize how big de-thatching is in the youth culture!) There are many reasons we can give for not doing what God wants us to do.

Four-letter words can be ugly! In fact, there is one that really bothers me. I get after my kids all the time for saying it. I've even caught my wife saying it. And since I'm telling family secrets, I have to admit that I occasionally slip up and say this awful four-letter word myself. The word is "can't".

I hate that word. It is used as an excuse so often. We are told in scripture that God "is able to do above and beyond all that we ask or think". (Eph. 3:20) "Can't" is the wrong starting place. God can do more than we imagine.

---

[4] Philip Johnson, Darwin on Trial (Downer's Grove, IL: InterVarsity Press, 1993) and Wedge of Truth (Downer's Grove, IL: InterVarsity Press, 2000).

[5] Lee Strobel, The Case for a Creator (Zondervan: Grand Rapids, MI, 2004).

Perhaps God wants to do more through you than you have ever imagined. Come up with another excuse or, better yet, get involved in the miracles that God has for you as you go on an adventure of faith with him.

There is always a resource. Ephesians 3:20 says God "is able to do above and beyond all that we ask or think". But Paul tells us that for a reason. That reason is found in the rest of that verse, "according to the power that works in you". God always has the resources to overcome our excuses. Reluctant warriors like Gideon- or you and me- need to remember that.

God called Gideon a mighty warrior because he was providing the resources Gideon needed to fight the battles ahead. And God calls you to fight the battle of faith- but not alone. He goes with you into every battle, providing the strength and stamina you need to accomplish the victory.

I listened with rapt attention to a man tell about the terrible battle he faced with the death of his son. His voice crackled with emotion as he described the agonizing ordeal no father ever wants to face. He spoke of faith and of frustration and of fear. He told of praying and pleading and weeping. But he also said something else that has stuck in my heart ever since. He said, "I discovered, in my darkest hour, this truth- when God is all you have, he is all you need."

Oh mighty warrior, reluctant and hidden though you may be, come join the battle! God is big enough to use you despite your fears and uncertainties. He can see beyond your reluctance to your potential. And he will give you the strength and power to win the battles of faith he calls you to fight.

Chapter Three: God Uses Fearful People

While I still get a little nervous every time I stand to speak before people, it is nothing like those first preaching experiences. I used to be an emotional wreck before messages. I sweated profusely. Waves of nausea washed over me like the beach at high tide. My voice tightened to a high-pitched squeal delivered in rapid bursts and halting stutters. (That part hasn't changed much.) In short, I was scared to death prior to each message.

I thought it was just me. But, surprisingly, I find that many people are nervous when it comes to ministry opportunities. We are fearful of what others think. We are scared of rejection. We doubt our abilities. But the amazing thing is that God uses scared, nervous, fearful people all the time.

Gideon was told by God to tear down the altar to Baal in his city and to replace it with an altar to God. But because "he was too afraid of his father's household and the men of the city to do it in the daytime, he did it at night." (Judges 6:27) I understand exactly how Gideon felt, don't you? He worried about what the men of the city might think of him- or do to him- if he carried out such a radical agenda. He even worried about his own relatives- "his father's household".

Fear of the consequences of his obedience to God gripped his soul.

Face the Reasons for Fear

Just as Gideon was fearful to follow God's clear instructions, we are often fearful of doing what we know God wants us to do. We may be reluctant to get involved in ministry, to share our faith or to take a stand for God's truth.

If you sometimes fear to follow God wholeheartedly, if you are less than immediately courageous in carrying out God's plans- you are not alone. Many of us are fearful instead of faithful. Many of us are nervous to step out in faith and follow God's bold agenda. There are many reasons for our fear.

Fear of disapproval. Gideon was told by God to tear down the altar of Baal. But not all the men of the city approved of such a bold- and potentially dangerous- plan. So Gideon did his work at night when no one was watching. Fear of disapproval is a powerful force. What will my boss think if I get serious about my faith? Will my neighbors think I am a fanatic if I invite them to church? Will my classmates shun me if I am too committed to my Christian principles?

I've tried to apply a lesson from my college football days to this fear. At Wheaton College, our football team had chapel services each week. During one of those chapel services, a fellow player talked about playing for God's glory rather than the applause of the crowd. He encouraged us to do our best to please the Lord with our play and not just to please the stadium.

That concept was very freeing for me. I loved for the crowd or my coaches and teammates to encourage me. But there was only an audience of one whom I really needed to please. I wanted the Lord to be pleased with my effort and hustle. I didn't have to worry about the approval of others if

I was focused on pleasing God. Even if my best effort didn't please the fans or my coaches I could be assured my best effort pleased the Lord.

Your approval in life and ministry needs to come from only one person. If you do what you do to the best of your ability and for God's glory- well, nothing else matters much. You don't need the approval of your boss or classmates or family. You have the approval of the only one who really matters.

Now we "people pleasers" know it is easier to talk about overcoming our fear of disapproval than it is to do it. We want everyone to agree with us always. We want- sometimes crave- the applause of men instead of the applause of heaven. But sometimes we can only have the praise of one or the other. Either we please God or we please people. And with that choice before me, I know which applause I want.

<u>Fear of conflict</u>. Do you like the television news shows where two people are arguing and talking at the same time? They seem to think whoever talks the loudest and complains the longest wins. I get headaches just listening to them!

Arguments can be exhausting, conflicts painful. Why bother causing them? Better to just "go along and get along", right? Better to run from conflict than deal with its painful aftermath.

But, Jesus tells us when we follow him conflict is sometimes inevitable. Christians in many parts of the world understand this well. They face conflict simply because they love the Lord. Their commitment to Jesus causes them to be persecuted. But they know their suffering cannot compare to the joy of following the Lord and gaining eternal life.

Gideon faced the choice of obedience to God or likely conflict with men. Even his choice to tear down the altar under cover of darkness was not enough to keep him from the clutches of conflict. But, he decided that potential conflict with men was better than conflict with God. Given the choice of conflict with men or disobedience to God- choose conflict with man every time.

I am encouraged by the example of believers in persecuted countries. I have a friend named John Moldovan who suffered great persecution in Eastern Europe during the days of communism. He faced conflict because of his faith and his outspoken commitment to following Christ. He was imprisoned, tortured and eventually exiled from his homeland. But, he was faithful despite the conflict.

It was one hour by jeep from the nearest source of electricity. There was no running water in the village. There were no restroom facilities. My friend Abdoulaye lived in a small mud hut in this remote part of Burkina Faso, Africa. He had trusted Christ as his Savior just a year earlier and now he felt as though God was calling him to be a pastor. He would be the first pastor, as best we knew, in the history of his small people group. In this predominately Muslim village, Abdoulaye was starting a Christ-honoring church.

Abdoulaye's commitment to Christ was difficult. There was conflict with others. Many of his own family openly criticized his faith. But he was faithful despite the conflict.

The courage of John and Abdoulaye and others in the face of criticism encourages me. They faced adversity because of faith and yet stood strong. Their faith was greater than their fear.

Fear of blame. "Who made this mess?" I can still hear my mother's voice as she sought the culprit to another messy floor or broken vase. The culprit was often me, but I knew that with three brothers, if I held out long enough, someone else might receive the blame.

If you never try anything, you can't be blamed for much. That is the couch-potato philosophy. Never take risks, never make mistakes. Except, never taking a risk is a mistake. God calls us to boldness and great steps of faith.

I recently heard Rick Warren say that he expects leaders in his church to make mistakes. He doesn't want them to repeat mistakes, but if they never make a mistake they are never taking any risks or trying new things.

We need some holy risk-takers who will be willing to attempt great things for God even if it means making some mistakes along the way. We need some folks who fear complacency more than blame.

Fear of blame is the opposite attitude of many of the successful people I know. It seems as though many successful people don't mind at all accepting blame for failures. Successful people tend to accept blame and deflect praise. That is, if there is a mistake or problem in the organization, they immediately accept full responsibility. If there is success or accomplishment in the organization, they are quick to praise the other people who have participated instead of taking credit.

<u>Fear of the unknown</u>. Nothing is more frightening to me than the unknown. My imagination sees problems bigger, difficulties steeper and conflict stiffer than reality usually reveals them to be. Not knowing what will happen allows me to imagine the worst.

The Lord of the Rings movies and books tell the story of some creatures called hobbits who leave their country on an incredible adventure. One of the hobbits, a gentle soul named Sam, joins his friend on a long journey into the unknown. As he is about to leave his homeland, he suddenly stops. His friend asks him why he delays. Sam says, "If I take one more step I will be farther from home than I've ever been." And then with resolve, he takes a step forward and into the unknown future.

Many times God calls us into an unknown future. We don't know where the path we are following leads. We can't see the end of the journey or even know the twists and turns our path will take. But we know God has called us to go forward. Like the hobbit Sam we have to take that first step onto new ground. We have to trust God even when we can't see the final destination.

Some of life's greatest adventures await our journey into the unknown. God calls us to follow him on that journey to the unknown by faith. David had never been a king until he became one. Paul had never been a missionary until he became one. Gideon had never started a revolution until he took that first step and tore down an altar to a false God.

<u>Fear of failure</u>. Maybe it is the result of growing up with three brothers, but I hate to lose. With brothers, much of life is about competition- who is the biggest, who runs the fastest or who hits the hardest. Being on the losing end of those things is not that much fun.

Hating to lose can be a fine thing but there are two directions to which it may lead. It may lead to hard work and a commitment to excellence. But it can also lead to an unwillingness to try new things or to take any risks. After all, you can't lose if you don't compete. The fear of failure can be paralyzing.

Have you ever noticed, however, that failure can be a great teacher? Failure can be a little like that tough Junior High teacher that gives lots of homework and challenging exams. You might not like her at the time, but looking back, you see how much you learned from her.

Failure can cause us to question our assumptions and open our eyes to the truth. Failure can teach us to dig deeper and look more intently. Failure can teach us lessons we need to learn. Failure can even be the foundation for future victories.

Attempting great things means we risk failing. But we also face the possibility of real success. If we fail, we learn invaluable lessons. If we succeed, our faith is strengthened. The only real failure is not to try at all.

Fearful but Obedient

What I absolutely love about Gideon is that he was scared to death, but he obeyed God anyway! Think about it. It doesn't take much courage to obey God on the easy things. Anyone can obey God when it is convenient and popular. But to obey God when you are scared of the results, when your culture and family don't approve- that is something special.

I would sing my little heart out! My mind still pictures me as a young boy at church on Sunday morning. My crew cut hairstyle looked sharp with a little wax on the front to make it stand at attention. A multi-colored suit coat with a clip-on tie gave me "the look". We sang hymns and I belted out the familiar tune "Trust and Obey".

That song was a staple of church life for me. "Trust and obey, for there's no other way, to be happy in Jesus, but to trust and obey." I sang it out with my fellow church-goers completely unaware of how off-key we were or of the important theology we were learning.

What I was unwittingly learning from that hymn was the relationship between my faith *in* God and my obedience *to* God. I might not always understand God's will. I might not always like God's will. I might sometimes find God's will difficult to follow. But if I trust God, I will want to obey him.

It sounds funny to put the words "fearful" and "obedient" together doesn't it? My youngest brother, Dan, was telling me a story recently. He started the conversation by saying "My hairdresser was telling me the other day..." Immediately, I stopped him and blurted out, "Wait a minute! What did you just say?" He repeated, "My hairdresser was telling me..." "Stop!" I shouted. "Did you just say the words 'my hairdresser'?" I never thought I would hear the two words "my" and "hairdresser" come from the lips of one of my brothers.

My barber, my butcher, my banker- sure. But "my hair-dresser"? Never!

You might not expect the words "fearful" and "obedient" to go together either. Gideon was scared. His faith was weak. He followed God's command in the middle of the night instead of openly. But, he obeyed nonetheless. He was fearful and obedient.

I have to put "fearful" and "obedient" together often when I witness. There is something scary to me when it comes to telling another person how to trust Jesus Christ as their personal Savior. But when the Holy Spirit prompts me to share my faith I want to be obedient despite my fears. I want to trust and obey.

Fearful but Protected

Flash back with me to my freshman year in High School. I'm a scrawny little kid walking the upperclassmen infested halls of my school. It is intimidating under the best of circumstances. But these aren't the best of circumstances. There is a bully who delights in making my life miserable.

The bully is two grades and forty pounds ahead of me. He sports a mustache and an attitude. He eats scrawny freshmen like me for lunch. Spying me walking to class, he smirks hatefully, pounds me in the arm and tells me I'm stupid. I avoid eye contact and keep walking as I usually do in this situation. My arm stings- but not as much as my pride.

Fast forward to the next year. The bully is still in the hall-ways and still mean. I've grown but I'm still no match for him. Now, however, I no longer fear his malice. Suddenly, I have friends. Big, upperclassmen friends. I'm on the football team and the Senior Quarterback and his buddies take a liking to me. The bully could still pound me, but he fears the retaliation of the football players. The old bully tactics are out when it comes to me. He will have to pick on someone else. I'm still nervous around the bully, but I am protected.

Gideon is fearful of obeying God's command to tear down the idols in his community. He is nervous of the Midianites and their power. But he is protected by the love, loyalty and lessons of his father.

The love of a father. When the men of the city get up the next day they are deeply troubled. The altar to Baal has been torn down as have the Asherah poles. An altar to the Lord has replaced them. Their idolatrous ways have been upset not to mention the trouble this could cause them with the Midianites. They begin a fact finding mission to discover the perpetrator of this mischief.

A careful search uncovers the culprit. Though he did his work at night, someone spills the truth. Gideon son of Joash did it.

The verdict is swift. Gideon must pay for this transgression with his life. They call on Joash to bring out his son so they can carry out their flawed verdict. There is only one problem with the execution of their sentence. The love of a father stands in the way.

Joash speaks to the hostile crowd and says in affect, "Let Baal carry out his own revenge! If he is really a god he doesn't need any help from you. He should be able to handle this one on his own."

A loving father is not going to turn over his son to a lynch mob. He isn't going to betray his son for obeying God's direction. Joash grew up in Israel. He knows the prohibition on idolatry. He may have feared the crowd enough to compromise his worship but he doesn't fear them so much he will stop loving his son.

If you have given your life to Jesus Christ as your Savior the Bible says you have become God's child. He loves you as his very own. You may fear what the world may do to you but you can live in complete assurance that your Father in heaven loves you completely and eternally. You may be fearful but you are protected. Your Father will face every battle, every challenge with you.

Dads, you're to be a protector in your home. And your love for your family is the cornerstone of that protection. Your children may not have to fight off idolatrous vigilantes but they will have to fight off the dangers of peer pressure. Your sons will need protection from the easy availability of pornography. Your daughters will need protection from conformity to the lowly standards of our culture.

If you love your children you will fight these battles and others with them. You will want to keep them from the harm the enemy intends for them. You will want to teach them to stand and fight their personal battles but you will want to do all you can to guard them until they are able.

I meet young men and women all the time who carry the scars of life without a loving father. They grew up with an absent father or an abusive father or a distracted father. They had no man in their vulnerable years to encourage them and to discipline them. And often they are looking desperately for someone, anyone to fill that void.

If a magic wand could be waved that caused every father to faithfully fulfill his responsibilities to his children, the waving of that wand would instantly change the world for the better. Fathers would love their kids and stand in the gap on their behalf. Many of the social ills of society would be lessened. Lives, families and eternity would be changed.

The loyalty of a father. My loyalty as a father was tested during my children's adolescence. I took the great loyalty examination called "teaching your child to drive". My scores were shaky and I needed to be graded on the curve.

Well do I remember when my second daughter got her Learner's Permit. That meant she could legally drive with an adult in the passenger seat. She could drive a car on the mean streets of O'Fallon, IL. She was only fifteen, but she was driving around in the family car with nothing between her and automotive mayhem and destruction but me. And I am only a man!

I tried to be encouraging and positive about her driving but my nervousness overcame my optimism. My "helpful advice" bordered on panicky demands for course corrections. Her minor driving infractions sent me into impassioned sermons on "The Importance of Cautious Driving for all Believers" or "Defensive Driving and the Afterlife". I know my primary loyalty is to my daughter but I found myself wavering between greater love for her or for low insurance premiums. Being a father can be difficult!

Gideon's father showed loyalty to his son at a critical moment. He stood up against the Baal worshippers who wanted to take the life of his son. At great personal risk Joash challenged them- he even challenged their theology. "Let Baal plead his own case" he said. "If Baal is so great," suggested Joash, "let him take care of his own battles." At this critical moment, Joash remained loyal to his son and to the faith of his fathers.

A loyal father is committed to faith. What a blessing you leave to your children, parents, when you follow the teaching of God's word and live a life of trust in Jesus Christ. Your family is blessed when it sees your love for the Bible, your earnestness in prayer, your boldness in witness and your passion for worship.

A loyal father is committed to family. These men are faithful to their wives and treat them with respect. They spend time teaching, playing and listening to their children. They know that family time is valuable and are always looking for ways to strengthen those relationships.

A loyal father is committed to the future. They know they are preparing now for their sons and daughters futures. They raise their children with one eye on today and one on tomorrow. Groundwork is laid which prepares their children for every opportunity for success.

The lessons of a father. Fathers are teachers and life is their classroom. Joash taught his son Gideon many lessons along the way in life, some good and some bad. Gideon watched his father cave in to the pressures of his culture and erect an altar to the false god, Baal. But he also watched his father defend him at the critical moment when he tore the idol down according to the instructions of the Lord.

Dad, what lessons are you teaching your children? What are they learning from how you drive (have you ever noticed that everyone driving faster than you is a maniac and everyone driving slower than you is an idiot?) or how you relax (did you have to miss his ballgame for your golf?) or how you deal with problems ("daddy, why are saying your golf words to that idiot?")?

Dad, be ready for those teachable moments. Stand strong on the critical issues of moral purity and biblical values. Teach your children right from wrong and best over mediocre. Be prepared to teach the lessons of life to your sons and daughters. You just never know when they may be asked to break down an altar to Baal.

It may be surprising, but God uses fearful people to accomplish his purposes. Perhaps you have some trepidation about involvement in ministry or service in your local church. Maybe you are frightened at the prospect of sharing your faith with a co-worker. It could be you are nervous about turning control of your schedule or pocketbook to the Lord. Well, fine. You are in just the right spot to be used by God to change the world!

Chapter Four: God Uses Cautious People

Each book is nearly 1,000 pages long and there are *three* of them. But, I determined to read them all. I'm talking about Shelby Foote's massive historical trilogy on the Civil War. One of the many interesting people he noted in his books is the Union General George B. McClellan.

General McClellan was an intriguing man. He was incredibly gifted at war preparation. He drilled the Army of the Potomac until they were expert marchers. His efforts at getting supplies and material in order were unparalleled. He was an outstanding planner and was extremely popular with his troops. In short, he seemed to be extraordinarily capable at everything needed of a general with one exception. McClellan was invariably cautious.

It seemed to Commander-in-chief Abraham Lincoln that McClellan was always preparing for war, but never waging it. He was planning and plotting attacks, but slow in their execution. Plans for attack were continuously delayed. On one occasion, Lincoln told McClellan that if the general did not want to use the army he would like to borrow it for a while.[6] Do you think anyone might say to us one day, "Hey, if you aren't going to use your faith I would like to borrow it for a while"?

I wish all believers were filled with faith. It would be great if we always followed God immediately. Don't you wish our response to the radical call of discipleship was always unhesitating obedience? Don't you wish we jumped at the chance to slay the giant like David or to step out onto the water like Peter? I would love that kind of faith. But, while I want my faith to be that strong, I have to admit that I am very grateful that God uses cautious, nervous, small-faithed people like I sometimes am.

Gideon could be a little on the cautious side of faith. He wasn't always aggressive and bold. Many of us can relate to that. Through personality or experience we often become tentative when God calls us to boldness. Whole churches can live by caution and not by faith.

First Baptist Church of Corinth, Texas was growing rapidly. The church was one hundred years old, but the expansion of Dallas had finally reached the little community and the only church in town was growing steadily. I had been the pastor of the church for a few years and we were excited about our future. Already bigger than we had ever been in our history, we believed the best was yet to come. We had, however, a couple of severe limitations.

First of all, we only owned one acre of land. With the need for parking alone, that is quite limiting. Secondly, we were now out of space. We had already begun multiple services to try to alleviate the crowding. Thirdly, the land around us was expensive. We were located on the interstate and the land around us was priced at $250,000 per acre. We had very limited resources and could not pay that much for land.

---

[6] Shelby Foote, *The Civil War: A Narrative: Fort Sumter to Perryville* (New York: Vintage Books, 1958), 240.

As we contemplated what our church needed to do to face the future with faith, we celebrated our 100 year anniversary with a special service. We invited former members and pastors back and made it a really special day of celebration. During the festivities, one of the former pastors took me aside and told me a story about our past.

The pastor said that some years before, the church had been growing. The community was just beginning to slowly grow as the urban sprawl began to creep their way. A man connected to the church owned the ten acres of land next to the church, right on the interstate. He was willing to sell it to the congregation for $20,000 for all ten acres. The church had that much money in the bank. The pastor said he urged the congregation to purchase this prime real estate. But, some of the church leaders nixed the idea saying, "We need to save our money for a rainy day." The pastor pleaded with them saying, "It is raining all around us now!" But, his pleas were to no avail.

I looked back at the records of our church. From that time of caution, the church began to slowly decline. Each year the church was a little smaller. By the time I arrived some thirteen years or so later, the church had 19 people in Sunday School, no conversions for almost two years, one acre of land and no money left. At a moment that called for bold faith- or even just moderate faith- the congregation chose caution.

Our growing congregation eventually chose to relocate and to continue to reach people. It was difficult and challenging, but God blessed our faith and the church grew incredibly. Some of the longest term members took the greatest lead in that step. But, we couldn't help but wonder on occasion what might have been if all those years before there had been a little less caution and a little more faith.

Caution can be an impediment to the great steps of faith God calls us to exercise. But, I am very grateful that God can use us even when we are slower to obedience than we need to be.

Beware caution in the face of the enemy

George McClellan was not the only general, North or South, who was overly cautious during the Civil War. Often, the strength of the enemy forces was overestimated and the potential for disaster over inflated. Once in a while, however, some highly zealous commander stepped out in some daring raid that was tactically unsound only to be thoroughly thrashed. This merely fed the cautious nature of any leader with a tendency to passivity.

One can understand the caution of a leader in battle. The consequence of misjudgment in such circumstances is often death or dismemberment. Even the stout-hearted can take pause when an enemy army is arrayed against them.

Gideon found himself facing enemy forces as a result of his obedient response to God's call. His step of faith in attempting to throw off the yoke of Midianite bondage led to an enemy camped at his doorstep. Judges 6:33 says "All the Midianites, Amalekites and Qedemites gathered together, crossed over the Jordan, and camped in the Valley of Jezreel."

Listen, when you have all the Midianites, Amalekites and Qedemites against you- well, those are a lot of "ites"! A person can get kind of cautious with all those enemies running around causing mischief.

Many a young church leader has started out with great faith and large dreams only to discover some "ites" arrayed against him or her. Someone says, "We've never done it that way before" and squashes the ambitious evangelism plan. Someone else says, "It costs too much" and puts an end to the new ministry. Another says, "We tried that before and it doesn't work" and squelches the outreach program. Caution begins to set in.

Maybe that young leader takes a bold step of faith only to discover great resistance. The metaphorical Midianites, Amalekites and Qedemites always rise up against faith. And often in the face of these enemies, God's people respond not with greater faith, but with greater caution.

You can understand that can't you? Don't you know that every step young David took towards Goliath only made the giant appear larger? The sword in Goliath's hand might look large at a distance, but it was downright massive up close and personal. Facing giants or Midianites practically screams out for a cautious approach. David chose faith. Gideon chose faith mixed with caution.

Remember the antidote to caution: a Spirit-filled life

I love the descriptive phrase of Judges 6:34. "The Spirit of the Lord enveloped Gideon." That means Gideon was completely surrounded by the Spirit. He was following God's direction and living by God's word. The presence and power of the Holy Spirit was surrounding Gideon and he was guided by faith and not by fear.

When our lives are yielded to the Holy Spirit we have an infusion of faith. Some people say the sign of being filled with the Spirit is speaking in tongues. I respectfully disagree. I think the book of Acts teaches that the sign we are filled with the Holy Spirit is boldness in our witness for God.

Over and over, the disciples- often fearful and cautious in matters of faith- become bold in their witness when filled with the Spirit. Peter denied he knew Christ before a little girl prior to the crucifixion. But, under the power of the Holy Spirit, he boldly risked imprisonment and death for his faith.

When my will is fully submitted to the Lord- another way of saying I am filled by the Holy Spirit- faith becomes my natural response. Then I am able to follow God boldly. In my own strength, I may tend towards fear. Under God's power, I live by faith.

Enveloped by the Spirit of the Lord, normally cautious Gideon takes a great step of faith. The Bible says "he blew the ram's horn". (Judges 6:34) The ram's horn is called a shophar and is way up towards the top of the cool Bible things- at least on my list. The shophar is a hollow ram's horn that has a hole cut in the end. It is usually a big curly horn that makes a distinctive, rich bugle sound. The Israelites blew the shophar on the Day of Atonement in the jubilee year to signify the release of slaves and debt. But it most often was used to call the people to battle.

I determined when I was visiting Israel once that I needed to buy a shophar. (You never know when you are going to need to call together an army!) I saw a beautiful one in one of the shops. It was long and perfectly curled. The problem was the shopkeepers wanted the gold of Solomon as payment. I put the horn back and suggested to my wife that instead of buying it we could raise our own ram in the backyard. She said she would get back to me on that one. She should be getting back to me any time now!

When Gideon blew the shophar to call Israel to prepare for battle against the enemy, the Abiezrites responded. Gideon's own tribe, previously fearful, found courage in the Spirit-led leadership of Gideon and responded in large numbers.

Gideon sent messengers to the surrounding regions calling for troops willing to stand against the enemy. And, under the Spirit-led influence of Gideon, many people responded. The same Israelites who had been hiding in "mountains, caves and strongholds" out of fear of Midian now responded in great numbers to Gideon's call to faith.

All that was needed for the people to turn from fear to faith was one man, led by the Spirit of the Lord, to set the example and take the lead. This parallels the story of David and Goliath. The faith-filled example of David in standing up to Goliath led the entire Israelite army to a rout of the Philistines. One person, filled with faith, can make a difference for others. One example of faith is all that is needed for others to follow.

You could be that man or woman. You could live by faith and stand boldly for the Lord. Your unflinching faith in the face of opportunity could turn the tide and lead to spiritual victory. You could boldly share your faith with others and minister to people in Jesus' name. What you need to accomplish that is a Spirit-filled life.

Evangelist D.L. Moody once heard a fellow preacher named Henry Varley say, "The world has yet to see what God can do with and for and through a man who is fully consecrated to Him". Moody was moved by that thought and kept repeating to himself, "Varley was talking about any man. He didn't say he had to be educated or scholarly. Just a man. Well, by the Holy Spirit in me I'll be that man."[7]

The same Holy Spirit who filled and empowered D.L. Moody in the nineteenth century is the same Holy Spirit who filled Gideon centuries before Christ. The same Holy Spirit wants to fill you and empower you for ministry. God's power available to us through the Holy Spirit is the key to living a life of faith instead of fear.

I love it when people get this! It's awesome when Christians finally understand that God can work through them and can accomplish great things through their lives. When they understand the power of the Holy Spirit who is available to fill and empower them, a new level of faith is

---

[7] John Pollock Moody: A Biography (Grand Rapids: Baker Books, 1995) Quoted in the Introduction by Luis Palau, 13-14.

reached. They gain a new courage to share God's love with co-workers and classmates. They trust God with the circumstances of life. They face life with a new confidence in God's ability to conquer the world's obstacles.

You could be the man or woman God uses to launch the next spiritual awakening. Your faith could be the launching pad for a great work of God in your family, your church, your nation or your world. A life "enveloped by the Spirit of the Lord" can do great things for God's glory. A life "fully consecrated to God" can accomplish much in winning the spiritual battles of this world.

Beware the easy return to caution

It is easy to return to form. Even after a great leap of faith, Gideon found it very simple to return to his old, cautious nature. His foray into the Spirit-filled life of faith was significant, but it didn't totally eradicate his tendencies of self-doubt and fret. After responding to God's call to battle with obedience, then boldly calling the people to join him- Gideon slipped back into the worried, nervous, "what if it all goes bad" mode he was in when the messenger of God found him hiding in the wine vat.

Old fears are familiar fears. The recovering alcoholic must fight to avoid the return to the bottle. The former drug addict can easily slip back to the old ways. It's simple for the formerly cautious to stop climbing the mountain of faith and instead slide back into the valley of fear and inaction.

Part Two: God Stretches People in Surprising Ways

Our aching muscles begged us to stop, but our coaches demanded more. We had to run farther, lift more and work harder than we thought was possible. Those coaches knew that we could do more than we thought, so they pushed our tired bodies to new limits. They stretched us beyond what we thought we could do.

I saw my old buddy Tom Johnston the other day. Tom teaches evangelism classes in a seminary today. But I knew him from college football days. During spring football at Wheaton College, our team did special drills to train us for the coming season. One of the drills was to run up the stadium steps... *with someone on our back*!

Somehow I ended up teamed with Tom. Now Tom outweighed me by a good 30 pounds or more. So, when he lugged me up the steps it was bad, but when I lugged him up the steps it was ridiculous! When I saw Tom recently, I reminded him of that terrible ordeal. As painful as those training sessions were, they prepared me for the strains of the season to come. Our coaches wanted to stretch us beyond the normal to make us the kind of players we could be.

One of the amazing things God does with those he loves is to stretch them. He takes them out of their comfort zones and calls them to new heights of obedience and service. He puts them in difficult positions in order to teach them and to grow them. From the valleys of challenging problems to the mountaintops of new ministry opportunities, God spiritually stretches his followers to make them more effective in service and Christ-like in character.

Romans 12:1 tells us "not to be conformed to the pattern of this world but to be transformed". God's stretching is designed to change us from conformity to the patterns of our culture and to conform us to his image and purpose. He doesn't want us to grow too comfortable with our current condition. Instead, God challenges us to become everything he wants us to be- everything we can be when we are following him fully.

God uses many devices to stretch us- not the racks of medieval torture chambers- but devices nonetheless. He uses difficulties and problems. He stretches us through challenges and obstacles. But God's stretching is done with the purpose of making us all we were created to become.

Chapter Five: God Stretches People through Dependence

Don't try this at home! In the old days some people used a dangerous approach to swim lessons. They threw the poor swim candidate into the pond and told him to swim. If he thrashed around and made it back to shore he was an official swimmer. If he didn't make it, well, at least they didn't have to worry about those difficult follow-up lessons!

God doesn't throw us into deep waters not sure whether we can make it, of course. He knows our abilities far better than we do. But God is not against putting us in difficult positions which can teach us to trust him.

I heard a seminary President talk about sending his students on mission trips. They went to some of the most difficult areas in the world. Someone asked him why he would send students to such dangerous places. The President answered, "I send them to those places because I can't find places that are more dangerous to send them!"

God wants us to learn to depend upon him and not on ourselves. So he sometimes puts us in positions where we can depend upon no one but him. There are times in life where we cannot depend on our abilities, talents, quick wit or sharp tongue.

Such was the case for Gideon. Gideon had an army of 32,000 men gathered for battle against the Midianites. That was still far fewer than the army of Midian, but it was a formidable force nonetheless. But God was not done stretching Gideon. He had some important lessons to teach him and the first step in the stretching process was to teach Gideon to totally depend upon God.

God Removes the "Brag Factor"

One of the little girls in our church recently announced to her mother that she was a genius. She read something in a magazine that told the characteristics of a genius and decided that she fit those characteristics adequately. The only problem was that the little girl had only read the word and had not heard it spoken. She didn't know the first letter of genius was a soft "g" sound like a "j" and that the "e" was the soft sound instead of the long "e" sound. So, instead of pronouncing it like "jee-nius", the little girl announced to her mother that she was a "ge-ni-us". Mispronouncing the word took away some of the impact of the statement!

Maybe you are some kind of "ge-ni-us". Perhaps you have great talents and gifts. But even those are gifts that God has given you and not something you can brag about.

God's words to Gideon are recorded in Judges 7:2. He says, "You have too many people for me to hand the Midianites over to you, or else Israel might brag: 'I did it myself.'"

That must have been disconcerting to Gideon. Gideon had gathered 32,000 men for battle. That was a lot of soldiers. But that was far fewer than the 135,000 warriors who were ready to fight for Midian. Midian could leave 100,000 men on the sidelines and still outnumber Israel.

God wanted Gideon, and all Israel, to learn to depend on him and not on abilities or military might. He didn't want them to brag to the folks back home, "I did it myself." So God told Gideon to tell his soldiers they can go home if they are "fearful and trembling". Listen, if you are looking at the situation militarily you might well be fearful and trembling. Your army is outnumbered almost 5 to 1. Those seem like bad odds!

The Bible tells us that 22,000 soldiers took advantage of this "get out of the army free" card. They had to admit they were afraid, but at least they were off army rations!

Only 10,000 remained. Large numbers of the very people Gideon was counting on just packed up and went home. Even the professional soldiers didn't trust Gideon- or the Lord.

Okay, at least all the malcontents were gone. There were still 10,000. The numbers were low, but these were the cream of the crop. Only the most dependable remained and perhaps there was still some hope.

But God said 10,000 soldiers were still too many. God wanted no one to think that the power of the army won the victory. He wanted to completely remove the brag factor. Gideon and the people of Israel must get to the place where they relied completely upon the Lord.

God was serious about removing the brag factor from Israel. But he doesn't stop there. He wants to remove the brag factor from our lives as well. He wants us to recognize that while God uses us to accomplish victories, victories are impossible for us to accomplish without God.

Sometimes we Christians are prone to bragging. We can begin to think that God is lucky to have us. But the truth is there is nothing we can do in our own power that has any real lasting value. I cannot save anyone from their sins. Only God can do that. I can't change lives and families and eternity. God does those things. My attitude should be one of gratitude that God allows me to participate in his work rather than thinking of myself as indispensable to God's work.

When I am most dependent upon God, I am strongest. When I am most dependent upon myself, I am weakest.

God often uses events to teach us some humility. My sixth grade son had a Christmastime "white elephant" gift exchange at the bible study class he has at our church. The students were to each bring a small gift to exchange with other students at the party and the teacher suggested that humorous gifts were a great idea. So, somehow my son and wife got the bright idea that giving a copy of my first book would be a funny gift to bring.

Now, I can see how there is some humor in my son bringing a copy of his father's book to the class gift exchange. But another part of me thought, "What greater gift can a boy or girl get than a copy of my book? What an honor it will be for them to receive such a fine gift this Christmas season! This will be better than a video game!"

The teacher, however, took all my pride away when she told me what happened at the party. She said that the gift she ended up with was a roll of toilet paper someone had unfurled, written scripture verses on, and then re-rolled. One of the little girls in the class ended up with a copy of my book. When the party ended, however, the little girl spoke to the teacher. She said, "Teacher, I don't want this thing. Will you trade me your toilet paper for this old book?" That is the kind of story that warms an author's heart, I can tell you that! Traded for toilet paper!

God wants humility from his followers and bragging about accomplishments is not allowed. God is careful to work on any semblance of pride and self-sufficiency that may be bubbling beneath the surface of our lives.

God was so concerned about Israel bragging about winning the victory over the Midianites that he made another military cut. Ten thousand was still too many, so God gave another test.

God had everyone get a drink of water from the brook. Some knelt to drink and some lapped water from their hands. Those who knelt were sent home and those who lapped, stayed. Only 300 men were left after this test.

Much speculation has occurred about the nature of this test. Was it just a means of separating the two groups or was there a greater reason? Some think that those who knelt down to drink were not prepared for an attack of the enemy while those who lapped from their hands were ready at a moment's notice. Perhaps this is why they were chosen to remain and to directly participate in the great victory which was to follow.

I'm not sure the reason for the selection, but I do know this. God uses people who are ready to be used. I Peter 3:15 tells us to "always be ready to give a defense to anyone who asks you for a reason for the hope that is in you." He wants us always ready to be an instrument he uses to accomplish his purposes.

I don't always know when I will have an opportunity to share my faith with a lost person, but I am to always be ready. I don't always know when I will have an opportunity to minister in Jesus' name, but I am to always be ready.

Granted, I don't know everything there is to know about warfare, but whittling the army down to three hundred men seems like an unusual way to fight a numerically superior force. How can an army of three hundred hope to stand a chance against a force of 135,000 men? No matter how well-prepared and ready for battle the three hundred may be, they can be no match for such a massive enemy.

A friend of mine was the president of a small seminary in the Midwest. He noted that they had few students, a small faculty and little endowment. That, he said, put them in a great position to be used by God! God often delights in using the weak things of this world to accomplish great things.

When God accomplishes great things with limited resources bragging is not an option. We can't take credit. We can't build our pride. We can only recognize that God is the author of the victory. Instead of bragging, we are left with humility.

We Move from Partial Humility to Total Dependence

God certainly wants our humility. But he wants something more than simply humility. Not only does the Lord want us to recognize that we cannot accomplish things of lasting value on our own, he wants us to reach the place where we understand our utter and complete dependence upon him. God wants to stretch us by teaching us to trust him completely.

How often have we tried partial dependence? You know that kind of attitude don't you? I'll depend upon God when things are really bad, but normally I will depend upon my own abilities. I'll just call on God when things are really bad or when I have already tried and failed. But God wants us to depend upon him completely, not partially.

There is a great difference between partial and complete dependence. I partially depend on a canoe. If my canoe springs a leak or overturns on a float trip I wade or, at worst, swim a few feet to the bank. There are other boaters on the river to assist. I have a life vest for the most difficult scenarios.

I recently read a book on Christopher Columbus. His dependence was not partial. Columbus completely depended upon his ship. The crew could not swim to shore should there be a mishap. He had no Coast Guard to call for help. There were no cell phones to call for help had there been a Coast Guard. And there were no cell phone towers had there been cell phones to call for help had there been a Coast Guard!

If the ship failed in the middle of the ocean, the lives of the crew would be lost. That is total dependence.

God whittled the army of Israel down so they would depend upon him and not upon their own power. He wanted them to recognize his power for victory rather than trusting in their own abilities.

Many of us trust our own abilities more than anything. We place our faith in our brains, our resources or our experience. Those things are, of course, gifts which God gives us. We are to use those abilities. I'm not advocating that we throw our hands into the air and say, "God, I will do nothing at all. I'll depend upon you and do nothing for myself."

You are to take responsibility for your choices and do the best with the gifts God gives you. But there is a difference between trusting yourself and trusting God. When you trust yourself, God is an afterthought or a last resort. When you trust God, you recognize that even your abilities are gifts from God. You can do nothing without God's blessing. You know that God can get along just fine without you, but you are beyond hope without God.

Depending upon God does not remove my responsibility. It puts my responsibility in perspective.

Success in my life is not determined by my ability-certainly not in God's eyes. God is the giver of my ability. My responsibility is to use those talents which God gave me for his glory while recognizing they are from God. Even my ability is dependent upon God. Success in my life is determined by my willingness to trust and depend upon God and his plans for my life.

God sometimes stretches us by putting us in a position where we cannot depend upon our talents. Many times I have spoken to people who were forced by the circumstances of life to stop depending upon themselves. They may have faced a tragedy too great to face alone. Or maybe it was a problem too large for them to handle without God. They found, in those difficult days, that they could rely on no one but the Lord. And they found him to be faithful.

I heard a committed Christian tell of a physical problem which led to a battery of medical tests. The tests showed that he had two possible problems. One was life altering; the other was life ending. For a period of a few weeks, while waiting for a further test, he was left with the uncertainty. Is it life altering or life ending? During that dark time he considered the foundation of his life. He said it like this, "I went to the bottom of my life and found it firm." His foundation of faith was solid.

God put Gideon in a position where he could depend upon no one but God. He couldn't depend on his country, his army or himself. He was absolutely dependent upon God. But he discovered, in that difficult day, that God was faithful.

I spoke to my friend Preston Nix who teaches at New Orleans Baptist Seminary. Hurricane Katrina struck just a couple of weeks after he and his wife and his little girls arrived. He and his family lost almost everything. They got out with a few clothes and their little puppy. They lost everything else under an avalanche of water and mold.

All his notes, all his books, all his pictures- almost everything he owned was destroyed and he was left with nothing but his family. (And that yappy little puppy!) The family was forced, in ways hitherto unknown, to depend upon God. But the testimony of my friend is that his faith in the faithful God of his salvation is greater than it has ever been.

Do you trust God? I know what you are supposed to say here. But do you really trust him? The testimony of Gideon is that if you will depend totally upon the Lord, you will find him to be totally dependable.

Chapter Six: God Stretches People through Insights

My son decided I needed to get my body more limber. So he led me through some stretching exercises. Not just one stretch. Many, many stretches. My son learned different stretching exercises from karate classes and baseball practices so he had a bevy of different, and often painful, ways to improve my flexibility.

God uses many different devices to stretch us. One of the important ways we gain spiritual flexibility is to develop our spiritual insight. God allows us to see new perspectives which change the way we view our lives.

I never got to watch "The Wizard of Oz" as a boy. It was always shown on Sunday nights and I was always in church on Sunday nights. So, for many years, I missed out on this enormously popular movie experience. From commercials, I knew the general gist of the story and that they had those creepy flying monkeys. (Those monkeys and the maniacal laughter of the wicked witch kept me from a good night's sleep for a week or two!) In more recent years, I've been able to watch the movie. (But I'm still creeped out by those monkeys!)

"The Wizard of Oz" started out in black and white. There were no colors in the early stages of the movie, just different shades of gray. But, when Dorothy stepped into the land of Oz, suddenly the entire movie dazzled with color. There were bright colors everywhere. And the whole idea of color television was a big deal back in those days. (Kids, we didn't even have video games back in those dark ages!)

The perspective change brought on from the sudden change from black and white to color was enormous. The gray of Kansas transformed into the sparkle of Oz.

God grants us insights into his power, his glory and his ability which dazzle our feeble minds. We discover God is far bigger and far greater than we have realized and our perspective on life and problems and opportunities is transformed.

Every Tuesday night I was in inner city Chicago. During college years I was involved in a ministry which paired college students like me with students in the projects on the South side of Chicago. I tutored a couple of young men in their school work and served as something of a mentor.

In some ways, God used me to stretch those young men. I remember asking my students- about second or third graders- to draw a map of the United States. They drew a big blob which stood for Chicago and a small little area which represented the rest of the country. I showed them a full map of the United States and how big it was in comparison to the small little area of their city.

In many other ways, however, God used those young men to stretch me and to give me a new perspective. I grew up white. I grew up in a white home, with white relatives and white neighbors. My life was highly Caucasian. I rarely met people who didn't have the same ethnic and social background. In the projects, there were no white people except when I and some of my fellow college students were there.

It was different to be in the minority. It was different for people to look at me and stare or ask me what I was doing there. It was different to be an obvious outsider. God used experiences like that to help me understand people of different backgrounds and races. I was stretched by opportunities like that. I gained new insights into other cultures.

Gideon needed to be stretched. God wanted to expand his mind and his spiritual reasoning. He needed to see some new perspectives and gain some new understanding. God especially seemed interested in helping Gideon expand his understanding of God's nature and power.

So, God gave Gideon some important insights into his character which would serve Gideon well. He expanded his perspective on God in at least three areas.

Insight one: God knows the way. Poor Gideon must have wondered if God knew what he was doing. He cut Gideon's army down from 32,000 to only 300 men. Is that any way to fight a war? Did God really know the right way?

God granted Gideon a new insight into his plans and ability. There on the side of a mountain, overlooking the great army of Midian camped in the valley below, God spoke to Gideon. God said, "Get up and go into the camp, for I have given it into your hand." (Judges 7:9)

Notice the use of the past tense. "I have given it into your hand." It's already a done deal. God was reassuring Gideon that he knew what he was doing and he knew how it would work out. In fact, from God's perspective, it was already worked out. God had given the Midianites to Gideon and his ragtag army of 300.

God uses past tense with us as well. He says, "You have been saved". Not just that you will be saved when you stand in God's presence one day. If you have trusted Jesus Christ as Savior and Lord, you have already received the promise. Heaven is already assured. Forgiveness is already guaranteed. While you may not see it all in present tense yet, the promises of God are so real that they can be stated in past tense.

I'm glad to know God knows what he is doing and where he is going. I don't always know the right direction. I don't always see how it will work out. But God has it under control.

I got lost. I got so lost that I had to do what all men fear to do. I had to stop and ask for directions. Actually, I did what most men in my situation try to do. I made my wife go in to the gas station and ask for directions.

In my defense, I did get a set of directions. I went on the internet and got the directions from where I was to where I needed to be. Problem was, the internet directions were wrong. I guess Al Gore got some things wrong when he invented the internet!

If the direction giver is wrong you will end up in the wrong place. If the Lord doesn't know the way, well we are in trouble.

But God does know the way. He knows the way for your life and your future. He knows the best way for you to live, the right choices for you to make and the direction your life needs to follow.

If you don't trust God's directions you will try things on your own. You won't cut the army down to 300. You won't obey God's teaching on morality. You will make your own decisions about your career or your personal life or your finances.

And you'll get lost.

Did you ever sing the old hymn "Trust and Obey"? It had a catchy tune and a lot of truth. It reminded us that we should obey the Lord because we trusted him and that if we trusted him it was natural to obey him.

God said, "I have given it…" Open your eyes to a new insight. God knows what he is doing and where he is going. He knows the way. Choose the wise path and follow him.

Insight two: God is greater than my fears. I've already admitted my fear of flying monkeys. What are your fears? Losing your job? Failure? Rejection?

God told Gideon to go to the camp of the enemy. Then the Lord made this interesting statement, "But if you are afraid to go…" (Judges 7:10) God knew the heart of Gideon. He knew his fear, his anxiety. And God knows your fears. But the Lord wants to stretch us by reminding us that he is bigger than our fears. He can use us despite our fearful attitudes. He wants us to be courageous and follow his direction even when it leads us into fearful places.

Fear can grow over time. The dark shadows in the room of a child can grow into frightening monsters left to imagination. Small problems become great. Great problems become insurmountable.

I pulled a prank during my teenage years which became legendary among those of us who shared it. It involved an old, abandoned monastery.

Far into the countryside from our home was an abandoned monastery which was one of the scariest places I've ever seen. (They probably had flying monkeys there at one time!) A group of kids from our youth group decided to go visit it one night just to say we had done it. But a scheme began to grow in my sinister mind.

I suggested to the other kids that I was going to head back home. But, instead, I jumped into the back floorboard of my older brother's car without being seen and asked him to play along. We also had Patti in our car, a girl so prone to fright I feared it might cause permanent harm should she be left out of my plan.

In the cars ahead of us, the teenagers (including my younger brother, Don) talked with great anticipation of the scariness of the monastery ahead. A crazy, old monk, it was said, often roamed the crumbling buildings at night.

The seed of fear was planted.

When we got the to bottom of the long, dark hill which led up the monastery, my older brother suggested all the cars go on ahead and turn around "just in case something happens".

The seed of fear was germinated.

As the others turned around, I jumped out of my older brother's car unseen and walked in the dark up the hill towards the abandoned old building.

I don't mind telling you that I was pretty scared to be up there by myself. A lonely owl hooted hauntingly. The wind eerily rustled the leaves. The only thing that kept me from panic was anticipation of what would soon transpire.

The crowd of teenagers was at the bottom of the hill slowly making their way towards me. I could hear their nervous laughter. They all huddled around the only flashlight which was in the hands of my younger brother- all completely unaware of my presence.

As they climbed the hill to within 60 yards, I called out in my most menacing voice, "All must die!" The group froze. "What was that?" someone asked. I heard a few sobs. Then someone said, "Oh, it was only the wind." They came closer. When they got within 20 yards, I called out again, "All must die!" Then I began to scream and run wildly at them.

For just a half-second, the group was frozen, as though their legs were incapable of movement. Then, my younger brother broke their stupor with his cry of "Run, you idiots!"

The seed of fear was producing a bountiful harvest!

The next few moments were pandemonium. Screaming, weeping kids were running at breakneck speed back down the hillside. I saw the flashlight beam bouncing towards the road, then suddenly arc high into the air and go black. My younger brother had been running with it as fast as he could, tripped over a log and the light flew from his grasp to shatter on the ground.

Some of the boys got to the cars first and screamed for the drivers to leave. Who cared that some of the girls had not yet arrived!

And, poor Patti. She knew that I was the one who was scaring them. But she panicked anyway as she thought, "What if the crazy monk was there already, killed Doug and is now coming after us!"

When the group found out it was me all along, I thought they would be mad. Instead, they were so thankful to be alive, they were glad it was me. They didn't even mind, too much, the skinned knees and hyperventilation!

One of the stretching exercises God performs in us is to develop our understanding of the size of God compared to the size of our fears. Our fears may seem large and terrible. But God is far greater than our fears. He can handle our problems and insecurities. He is bigger than our worries.

Take a friend. God said to Gideon in Judges 7:10, "But if you are afraid to go to the camp, go with Purah your servant." Verse 11 says that is exactly what Gideon did. He admitted he was afraid to go alone and he took his trusted servant Purah with him.

That's all we know about Purah. He was Gideon's servant. And, at a critical moment in time, he was Gideon's strength.

It can be hard to go alone. Fears can be larger when faced alone. Enemies can appear more numerous. So, God told Gideon he could take a friend.

I cannot tell you how great it is to have friends. I need their concern, their insights and, sometimes, their courage. I have friends I can call at any moment about any need. But it isn't that way for everyone, I'm afraid.

Many a Gideon has to face life's challenges without a Purah by his side. Many Christians have no one to lean on and no one to face difficulties with. They live paralyzed by fear with no one to turn to.

If you are living a life a fear, one of the great things you can do is to find a friend. Find someone who knows the road you are traveling and ask them to come along. Find a small

81

group of fellow believers and share your heart with them. Become vulnerable. Admit your fears.

As our church has grown larger, we've battled with a real need. We know people need to know others and be involved in each other's lives. So, we are always encouraging people to join our small group Bible studies.

Many adults are reluctant to get into a small group. They can be anonymous in our worship services. But people know their name in small groups. They can sit in the back and stay uninvolved in a worship service. In small groups, everyone knows if they missed that week or if they stayed silent. It is easier to just attend the big worship service. But, they miss something if they don't get involved in the lives of others.

When people need ministry, they turn to their friends. When they have questions, they turn to their friends. When they are scared, they turn to their friends. But, if they never make a friend or become a friend- who do they turn to? Who turns to them?

Purah has only one cameo appearance in the Bible. When Gideon needed a friend, Purah was there. We need a few more folks like him. God uses folks like that to help us stretch our understanding of his greatness.

<u>Listen and learn</u>. God gave specific instructions to Gideon and Purah. "Listen to what they say, and then you will be strengthened to go to the camp." (Judges 7:11)

God wanted Gideon to listen to what was being said so he would see for himself that God was greater than his fears. So God had Gideon sneak down to the outpost of the camp of the Midianites and listen. He didn't have to do anything yet- just listen.

Listening is a great tool for learning. Note how often Solomon asks his son to listen to his advice and warnings in the early chapters of the book of Proverbs.

Prov.1:8- "Listen, my son, to your father's instructions."
Prov. 2:1-2- "My son, if you accept my words and store up my commands within you, listening closely to wisdom..."
Prov. 3:1- "My son, don't forget my teaching, but let your heart keep my commands."
Prov. 4:1- "Listen, my sons, to a father's discipline and pay attention so that you may gain understanding."
Prov. 4:10- "Listen, my son. Accept my words, and you will live many years."
Prov. 4:20- "My son, pay attention to my words; listen closely to my sayings."
Prov. 5:1- "My son, pay attention to my wisdom; listen closely to my understanding."
Prov. 5:7- "So now, my sons, listen to me and don't turn away from the words of my mouth."

Doesn't it seem that Solomon wants some listening from his sons? He has something to say and he wants his son to hear him.

God wanted Gideon to hear what was being said in the camp of the enemy. Gideon needed to know that it was the enemy who was scared and God who was at work.

I'm not sure I'm a very good listener. My wife said something about that to me the other day, but I didn't really catch it all. Wait a second. Was I supposed to take out the trash or something?

Listening to God's word is a really important part of God's stretching exercises. He wants to teach us and to build our faith. When we learn about his plans for us- eternal life, abundant life, power for effective ministry, peace that passes understanding- our faith grows deeper. When we discover that we are more than conquerors and that we are God's ambassadors and that we can come boldly into God's presence, our faith is built and strengthened.

Insight three: God has things under control. Football has a special play called the "trap play". At first glance, it appears at first to be a terrible idea for the offense. The offensive lineman doesn't even try to block the defensive lineman. The offensive lineman turns to block another man and just lets the defensive player go right by him.

It seems like a gift to the defensive player. The offense has messed up the play. No one blocks him and he has a free shot at the running back.

But if it is done right, at just the last moment, the defensive player discovers that the play was not messed up at all. A big old offensive guard from the other side of the line of scrimmage has left his normal blocking scheme and is smashing into the side of his helmet. He has been "trapped". The offense knew what it was doing all along.

It must have seemed like a busted play to Gideon. The Bible says the enemy "had settled down in the valley like a swarm of locusts". (Judges 7:12). The same verse said their camels alone were as numerous as the sand on the seashore. The enemy was bearing down on him and everything about the situation looked bad. But God knew what he was doing all along.

<u>Home of throwed rolls</u>. If I ever want to really eat a lot of "down home cooking" I know where to go- Lambert's Cafe, "home of the throwed rolls".

I've been to a couple of different Lambert's Cafes. If you have ever been there, you know that they dish out lots of food and they have a unique way of serving your bread. They throw it.

If you want a roll, some guy just wings one over to you from across the room. I always wanted to throw my food as a boy. These guys do it every day. This unusual service is so well-known that it is used as their advertising gimmick- "home of the throwed rolls".

Gideon got in on the original throwed roll. Only it wasn't a roll. It was a loaf of barley bread.

God allowed Gideon and his servant to eavesdrop on a conversation. At the edge of the camp, one of the enemy soldiers was talking to another soldier. The man had experienced a weird dream. It seems a loaf of barley bread came rolling down the hill into the Midianite camp. The loaf struck a tent and caused the tent to turn upside down and collapse.

That's a weird dream alright. I've had some strange dreams on occasion. I don't think I've ever dreamed of loafs of bread on the attack, however.

But what made the story most remarkable to Gideon was the interpretation of the dream given by the other soldier.

"His friend answered: 'This is nothing less than the sword of Gideon son of Joash, the Israelite. God has handed the entire Midianite camp over to him.'" (Judges 7:14)

Suddenly, Gideon was given a clear insight into what the enemy was thinking and what God was planning. He must have thought his small army was so small that the enemy was unafraid. Instead, this soldier was convinced that God was about to use Gideon to destroy the entire Midianite camp.

The barley loaf is cheap bread. It isn't some fancy pastry or glazed doughnut. It is just the common bread of life. But, in the dream, a roll of barley bread turned the whole tent upside down.

That was exactly God's plan for Gideon and his band of 300. They were just a small group compared to the great armies of the world. But God was going to use them to turn a mighty nation upside down.

It is encouraging to know God has everything under control. He isn't panicky or worried. We may be only small barley loaves to the world, but God knows what he can do with a roll.

I want to remind you that God can handle your world. He can handle your problems and your doubts. He is bigger than any enemy or obstacle you may be facing.

Perhaps God is stretching you right now. He is helping you to see that he is bigger than you think and he is bigger than your problems. He is giving you new insights into his ability and sovereignty. He is showing you that you can trust him and live by faith. He is reminding you that he can handle all the issues of your life and your future. He is stretching your understanding of his strength and power. He says to you, as he did to Gideon long ago, "Get up and go into the camp, for I have given it into your hand."

Understanding God's sovereignty is a stretch which every Christian needs. It is an insight from which every follower of Christ benefits. And it is absolutely essential for every warrior in hiding.

Chapter Seven: God Stretches People through Victories

Moral victories can only go so far. We needed a win. With three different coaches in three years, my college football team was struggling. We had new systems to learn and new coaches to teach them. Recruiting of new players and retention of current players had suffered with the upheavals. As a senior and team captain, I was especially frustrated with our losing streak.

I know you can learn a great deal in the times of adversity. I know you can learn things from losing. But, I was tired of learning lessons that way. I wanted to learn something from winning!

The losing streak continued. A missed field goal cost us one game. A dropped pass kept us from winning another. One team was only able to beat us- and this seems so unfair- because they scored five or six more touchdowns than we did!

We finally broke our losing streak with a solid victory and the atmosphere in the locker room and on the practice field changed dramatically. Everyone was happier. The tedium of workouts was lighter. The team was rejuvenated. The sky was bluer and the song birds sang sweeter. The locker room even smelled better. Success made us hungry for more success.

There is no question that you can learn a lot from adversity. You can be stretched by problems and by defeats. But God also stretches our faith by giving us spiritual victories.

Nothing charges me up more than seeing someone I know and care about come to faith in Christ. When I see the spiritual victory of salvation I am energized. My faith is strengthened and my spiritual resolve is deepened. And my insight into the greatness of God- his power to transform- is sharpened with new appreciation.

I recently baptized a young Air Force pilot. His wife gave her life to Christ many years ago. But he felt that he was self-sufficient. He didn't need God. If others did, that was fine. He didn't need anything else. He was smart, successful and talented. He would be just fine without giving control of his life over to God.

His wife prayed for him often. She even persuaded him to join her in worship on occasion. Their son attended our Christian school and he trusted Christ as his savior. He was baptized in our church. But dad, well, he just didn't need God in his life.

And then, one Sunday, God just broke through the stubbornness. God showed him that men are powerless to save themselves. Only by trusting in Jesus' death and resurrection can we have hope of forgiveness, eternal life in heaven and abundant life on earth.

I asked anyone in the congregation that morning who wanted to give their lives to Christ to join me in a "sinner's prayer". I led them in a simple prayer asking Christ to forgive them of their sins as they repented of them and giving control of their lives to the Lord. The wife told me she was praying for her husband as he sat beside her that morning- hoping he would turn his life to Christ. Her hopes, however, had been dashed many times before.

That afternoon, this Air Force officer told his wife about the amazing thing that had happened to him. He told her that during the service he prayed and asked Christ to come into his life. Everything on the inside, he said, had changed. He knew he was a new person- reborn spiritually. And he was as excited as he could be!

He told his friends and family about his new life in Christ. On that next Wednesday night he told me of his conversion and asked to be baptized. Soon thereafter I had the privilege of joining him in publicly professing his faith in Jesus Christ through believer's baptism. It was a moment I will never forget.

Moments like that serve to deepen my appreciation of God's grace. Watching a life changed by God's transforming power helps me appreciate the Lord's greatness and his goodness.

I know there is much for me to learn in the difficult times. Perseverance and patience are often learned most fully when victory is more distant. But I am so grateful for the spiritual insights which come during those wonderful, heady times of God-given success!

Victory comes with worship. Gideon came back from overhearing the enemy soldier's dream with renewed vigor. After hearing the dream of a loaf of barley rolling down the hill to destroy a Midianite tent and the interpretation that he and his army were going to destroy Midian by God's power, Gideon was oozing with confidence.

The first thing Gideon did was glorify God. The Bible says "he bowed in worship" (Judges 7:15). When he understood what God was doing, he could not help but give praise to God.

Confidence in God-given victory is a great motivation for worship. Nothing motivates us to worship God more than a realization of his great power to meet our great needs. God is not a limited, frail or weak god. He is Lord of lords and

King of kings. The more we recognize his sovereignty the more we will desire to bow in worship before him just as Gideon did.

Worship is very connected to victory. Christian churches across the world worship on Sundays because the victory of the resurrection was on Sunday. While worship recognizes our inadequacies and failures, it rejoices in the victory provided by God over those failures. Victory is at the heart of the gospel message and, therefore, at the heart of our worship.

Gideon grasped this concept. When God revealed the victory, Gideon bowed in worship. He praised the God who gives us victory over our enemies and our failures. He worshipped the Lord who uses barley loaves to steamroll the armies assembled against his people.

Worship can come in many styles. But always there is an underlying sense of victory- and therefore joy- in any true worship. Realizing the greatness and goodness of God is reason enough for us to rejoice in worship. Knowing that God has promised and provided the victory is always at the core of our adoration and praise.

<u>Victory comes through our activity</u>. With the promise of victory came new confidence. Gideon "returned to Israel's camp and said, 'Get up, for the Lord has handed the Midianite camp over to you.'" (Judges 7:15) The man found hiding from Midian in the winepress was now eager for the battle. Victory was assured.

Gideon urged the army to "get up". His worship was followed by action. True worship flows naturally into right action. Grasping the goodness and greatness of God leads to faithful service. We "bow in worship" then "get up" for service.

There is a terrible disconnect that has happened in much of the Western church. Worship and service have been severed. Rather than leading to a deepened commitment to obedience, worship is often seen as an end in itself. This is both tragic and heretical. If our worship does not lead us to right living it is not true worship- it might be emotionalism, it might be exciting, but it cannot be genuine worship if it doesn't lead us to obey our great God.

If there is no "get up" after "bow in worship" I doubt that there was any genuine worship to begin with. Our worship always leads to action just as faith without works is dead. What happens in Sunday worship ought to affect how we act at Monday work or Friday night activities.

Victory comes with our participation. While God could do everything he does without our help, he chooses to use us in his work. Every follower of Christ has a place, a pattern and a part.

You have a place. Perhaps the most famous portion of the Gideon story is the army's choice of weaponry. Gideon divided the army into three groups of 100 men each. He handed each soldier a trumpet and an empty pitcher with a torch inside. Not only was the army of Israel going to be vastly outnumbered, it was also relying on as unusual a choice in equipment as has ever been known in warfare!

There are television shows dedicated to showing the latest in warfare technology. They show the newest missiles, the most recent innovations in combat robots, the most sophisticated aircraft and such. It is amazing to see the incredible inventiveness associated with modern armed combat. In all those shows, I have yet to see a suggestion that armed combatants resort to the use of trumpets and torches. Maybe it is coming up in future episodes, but I haven't seen that strategy yet.

God's strategy for Gideon and the army is simple yet brilliant. It won't rely on superior numbers or weaponry. It will rely on the Lord and will build on the fear already gripping the hearts of the enemy.

Each of the 300 men had a place. Each had a job to do that no one else could do. Each had a trumpet and each had a torch.

<u>You have a pattern</u>. After giving each soldier a trumpet and a torch, Gideon said "Watch me and do the same. When I come to the outpost of the camp, do as I do." (Judges 7:17) Note that it wasn't "do as I say", it was "do as I do".

You parents know, don't you, that "do as I do" is always better teaching than "do as I say"? The example you set is far greater than the words you say. When Gideon said "watch me and do the same" he is speaking the reality of parents everywhere.

I heard the story of a golfer who had a young son who was already proficient at the game. The father was on the golf course with some friends and decided to show his friends how well he had taught his son the intricacies of the sport. He said to his son, "Son, show these fellows how I taught you to play the game." The young son immediately took out a club, shouted a profanity and threw it into the lake!

What you do is far more important to your leadership lessons than the words you use. Gideon understood that lesson and demonstrated to his soldiers exactly how they were to act and what they were to do. He said, "Follow my example, do what you see me doing, act as I act."

Some of you have great models of faith in your personal life. Perhaps your parents or grandparents lived out the faith and their example cried out to you "follow me!" But many of you have not had such an example- at least not from other people.

I'm glad that whether we have had good role models or not in friends and family, we can all know the example of Christ. He is our perfect pattern, our matchless model. I see in his life the image I am to strive for.

<u>You have a part</u>. Gideon told the Israelites to follow his example. When he blew his trumpet they were to blow theirs.

They were to shout "the sword of the Lord and of Gideon". They were to break their pitchers and let their light shine.

You have a part to play in God's kingdom that no one else can play. No one can take your place. We each blow our own trumpet, shout with our own lungs and let our light shine. Gideon could do his part. The soldier could do their part. I do my part. You do your part. We each have a role in God's work.

Our church has an orchestra which plays in some of our worship services and musicals. Imagine that you are in that orchestra. (Some of you will need to imagine real hard!) Let's make you our imaginary Oboe player. The Oboe is a beautiful instrument and you are the imaginary player in our imaginary scenario.

No one else in the orchestra can play the Oboe part for you. When the Oboe plays some harmony, only you can play. When the Oboe has the melody line, no one but you can play that part.

God has made you a unique part of his kingdom's work. No one else can play the melody and harmony lines God has given to you. God doesn't expect me to take your place. I have my own part. God doesn't expect you to take my place. You have your part. But victory comes because we each do our part in the symphony of life.

Victory comes from our witness. The Bible tells us in Judges 7:19 – 20 that the soldiers each "blew their trumpets and shattered their pitchers". They shouted "the sword of the Lord and of Gideon." That is it. That is all they did. They just blew their trumpets, uncovered their torches and shouted with their voices.

God brings victory through our simple witness. He asks us to use our voices, our abilities and our talents. He brings the victory, of course. But God uses our witness to accomplish his work.

One of our church member friends gave me a copy of a letter he'd just received. It was a thank you letter from a young man he met some years ago. The young man wrote in the letter of the events which let to his conversion.

My church member friend met this young man at a family funeral in another state. In their conversation, spiritual matters came up. My friend shared the basic message of the gospel with the young man. When he got home, he sent the young man a gospel tract and encouraged the man to trust Christ for salvation.

This began a spiritual journey for the young man. He began attending church, heard more of the message of faith. Eventually, he repented of his sins and gave his life to Christ. His fiancée soon trusted Christ. Then, his mother trusted Christ.

This young man wrote to my friend to thank him for the influence of that witness some years ago. My friend simply shared a witness of God's grace. But through that witness, God brought victory to at least three individuals.

God uses our simple voice, our trumpet call and our shining light to bring victory to a dark world. I'm so grateful God allows us to be part of his triumph over darkness by the use of our simple witness.

Victory comes beyond our abilities. The victories God gives to us are beyond what we can do. God does what only he can do. There is no way 300 men could defeat a vast army of 135,000 men. That is beyond man's ability. But it isn't beyond the ability of the Lord.

The Bible tells us that the Midianite army's response to the trumpets and the torches was panic. The army cried out and fled. In the confusion, the Midianites began to fight each other. In fact, the Bible says, "the Lord set the swords of each man in the army against each other." (Judges 7:22) God did what no man could do. God brought victory beyond the abilities of the Israelites.

Aren't you glad to know the Lord can do "above and beyond what we ask or think- according to the power that works in you"? (Eph. 3:20) Aren't you glad he is able when we are unable? God takes our ordinary abilities and does extraordinary things through them.

God uses victories to stretch us. He teaches us the lessons of faith and the power of his might. He reminds us of what he can do through us. He teaches us that we can be used to accomplish his awesome plans.

All you need is a trumpet, a torch and a voice- even if you are a warrior in hiding. Just give God the simple abilities you have. And then watch him use them- and you- to change the world.

Chapter Eight: God Stretches People through Criticism

"**N**o one likes a critic", the old maxim goes. I've got one just as universal. "No one likes to be criticized."

Criticism can crush us, motivate us, change us or teach us. It can be done with love, out of malice, with good or bad intentions. But God can- and often does- use criticism and even critical people in our lives to stretch us.

Everyone faces criticism and pastors are not immune. I've heard of pastors being criticized for the color of their tie, their spouse's singing voice (or lack thereof), the way they comb their hair and the age at which their children are potty trained! And there are no pastors in the world who don't have some who are critical of their preaching.

As a young man, I heard someone criticizing the preaching of Adrian Rogers, pastor of Bellevue Baptist Church in Memphis. He was often considered one of the finest preachers of his age. "What chance do my sermons have of being criticism-free if they don't like Adrian's sermons", I thought.

Since no one likes being criticized and everyone gets criticized, we might as well learn all we can from the experience. There are some questions we should ask ourselves when we face criticism.

The first question to ask ourselves when facing criticism is, "Is the criticism true, or even partially true?" If someone were to criticize my preaching as being obtuse, I would not like it very much. But my liking or not liking the criticism has nothing to do with whether or not the criticism is true.

If the criticism is true, or partially true, I need to know that truth. I cannot make the changes necessary to improve or change if I don't hear and understand the truth. If the criticism is untrue, or largely untrue, I can factor that lack of truth into my understanding and response. Remember, an unkind or poorly spoken criticism does not necessarily make the criticism untrue or unworthy of my attention.

A second question to ask is, "Does the criticism need to be opposed or ignored, or partially opposed or ignored?" Some criticism, if untrue, must be immediately refuted. "Pastor, you must be embezzling money" is such a serious charge that it must be immediately challenged and opposed. That would be a good time for an independent audit. (Unless, of course, you are embezzling money- in which case I counsel an immediate confession, resignation and an attorney!)

Some criticism is best ignored. Criticisms about things beyond our control or things which are insignificant fall into this category. Consider the source when deciding whether to ignore criticism or not. Silly people may say silly things but we are not required to pound them for each case of silliness.

A third question to ask is "What can be learned from this criticism?" This may be the hardest, but most important question asked. The lesson to learn may involve some changes God wants to make in our lives. The lesson may be to learn to trust God more deeply when we are unfairly attacked. Regardless of what the lesson is, if it is from the Lord it is important and beneficial.

A final question to ask is "What is the right way or the wrong way to react to this criticism?" Should I respond in kind? "Oh yeah, well I think you are pretty stupid too!" Or, does God want to use this event to teach me forgiveness? Does the Lord want to teach me graciousness in the face of adversity? Might he want to use this to correct some flaw in my thinking or even in my character?

Criticism was the first reward for Gideon after his defeat of the Midianite camp. Judges 8:1 records the response of the men of Ephraim after the victory. "The men of Ephraim said to him, 'Why have you done this to us, not calling us when you went to fight against the Midianites?'" The verse goes on to say, "And they argued with him violently."

What a greeting for the war hero! The men of Ephraim don't say, "Thank you Gideon for the great victory you won on our behalf." There is no, "Well done, Gideon. Your victory means wonderful days of freedom and peace are on the horizon- job well done!" Instead, "they argued with him violently" because they were not able to share in the glory.

Instead of gratefulness for Gideon's service to God and his country, these fellow Israelites are angry that they were not included in the battles- and the prestige which would surely accompany the victory. Instead of thankfulness, there is dissension.

It sounds like jealousy. It sounds like pride. It sounds like animosity. It sounds childish.

Dissension is a common problem. Ephraim is recorded in the Old Testament as causing dissension on more than one occasion. This tribe had a similar episode of dissension recorded in the twelfth chapter of Judges. It led to terrible bloodshed. Dissension, for Ephraim, had become a serious and repeated problem.

Why are churches and Christians in general so easily drawn to dissension? Why is complaining and "violent arguing" so commonplace in spiritual circles? Perhaps we allow more jealousy and pride and animosity and childishness into our lives than we care to imagine.

It was a cold day in Illinois, just a few weeks before Christmas. I was enjoying running some errands with my wife and daughter. We needed some things at Sam's Club-which was good for me because they have free food samples if you hit the time just right.

Being the gentleman that I sometimes am, I dropped my wife and daughter off at the front door so they wouldn't have to walk so far in the blustery chill. There was a stop sign by the front door, so I let them grab their things and pile out of the truck.

Then it happened. Someone behind me had the audacity to honk their horn! Apparently, the few seconds of waiting required for me to let the ladies out was more than this individual could take. So, he honked. I glared at the rear view mirror and stewed. I couldn't help but note the model and make of the "honker's" car.

As I parked my truck, I noticed the man exiting his car. For a moment, I contemplated fisticuffs. Had he been a large man I'm quite sure this idea would not have been so prevalent. But he was an older man and rather small. I thought to myself, "I can take him!" Wisely, I thought better of the idea. (Besides, the only thing worse than being beaten up by a large, young man is to be beaten up by a little, old one.)

I watched the man enter the store and thought again to myself about what a rude man he was. I recounted to my wife and daughter the terrible indignity of it all.

Later, I saw the same man in the store. His cart was blocking my access to a food sample. Now I was really steamed! I thought to myself, "Oh, sure, the guy's in a terrible hurry to get my truck out of his way, but I don't see that same concern to get his cart out of the way of my food needs!"

Once again I felt the need to regale my wife and daughter with the insensitivity of "the honking man" as he would henceforth be named. Oh, the unmitigated nerve of some people!

Shortly thereafter, as I munched on a sample of cheese-cake, a question came to me. Which man had more dissension in his heart- the one who honked once or the one who held the grudge for the next 30 minutes? Questions like that can bring some indigestion. (And so can too many food samples!)

Dissension comes easily to our hearts if we leave them unguarded. It seems there is an epidemic of dissension in churches today.

Today, as has happened far too many times in my ministry life, I spoke with a minister who was in a church embroiled in controversy. Sides had been drawn; anger had spewed. It wasn't over theology or moral indiscretion. It was, as it often is, over a personality conflict.

Maybe church conflict is not more common now than it used to be. Maybe I am just more aware of it now. But conflict in churches seems far too frequent and the reasons far too trivial. The dissension of the men of Ephraim seems much like the dissension so often seen in churches of this generation.

Gideon's response to the dissension of the men of Ephraim is serious diplomacy. When there is a fire, you can add gasoline to that fire and watch the blaze explode, or you can add water to the fire and cause the flame to dissipate. Gideon was a water thrower.

Gideon's response is recorded in Judges 8:2, "What have I done now compared to you? Is not the gleaning of Ephraim better than the vintage of Abiezer?" In effect Gideon was saying, "Listen, my small accomplishments can't compare to all the incredible things you fellows have done over the years. My little clan is nothing compared to your great tribe."

The humility in Gideon's reply is disarming. Instead of reminding Ephraim of his greatness, Gideon reminds them of how little he really has to brag about. Humility is so uncommon that it must have been surprising to the complainers of Ephraim.

In Judges 8:3, Gideon continues, "God handed over to you Oreb and Zeeb, the two princes of Midian. What was I able to do compare to you?"

Not only is Gideon humble about himself, he is exceedingly free with his praise of his antagonists. "Oh, sure," Gideon seems to say, "I may have started the battle, but look who captured the kings. You guys in Ephraim deserve the real praise!"

Gideon sounds like a diplomat. He does all he can to impress the host with his gratitude for their service while downplaying his own role.

The Bible records the reaction of Ephraim to Gideon's diplomacy. "When he said this, their anger against him subsided." (Judges 8:3)

Instead of a response in kind, Gideon is diplomatic and respectful. His reaction calms the troubled waters and eases the jealousies and tensions that threaten the fabric of the nation. Rather than escalating the rhetoric, his gentle answer softens hearts of his critics.

Gideon followed the advice of Proverbs 15:1which says, "A gentle answer turns away anger, but a harsh word stirs up wrath."

This story reminds us of several lessons- the danger of jealousy, the harm of dissension and the importance of kindness under pressure. Perhaps the greatest lesson to take from this criticism, however, is our need for dependence upon God.

Criticism, fair or unfair, can be used by the Lord in our lives. It can remind us of how much we need the Lord. It can cause us to trust Him more fully and not in our own abilities or even in our past successes.

God stretches us through the criticism. He keeps us from unhealthy dependence upon self. We are reminded that we cannot ultimately depend upon our abilities, our resources or even our friends. We really do need the Lord.

The great need for our land and our time is not victory over our problems. It is not a new program that brings greater success. It isn't the right political leaders or better economic situations. The greatest need we have is for a real revival in our souls.

When we trust in ourselves instead of the Lord, revival tarries. But when we trust in the Lord with all our heart, mind and soul, revival can come. God uses events, like criticism and uncertainty, to remind us of our need for him.

No one likes criticism. Some of you reading this are facing an unfair mountain of criticism right now and I know you don't enjoy it. But God is able to use criticism, even critical people, in our lives to bring good. We can learn to trust him more deeply and depend upon him more fully. And that is always a good thing.

Chapter Nine: God Stretches People through Adversity

I doubt there is any commodity which stretches people as deeply and thoroughly as adversity. Problems and difficulties, pain and calamity- these things stretch us more than perhaps anything God allows into our lives.

Steve Farrar speaks of adversity in his outstanding book <u>Tempered Steel</u>. He notes the way God uses difficulties. "God has designed hardships," he notes "to make you a better man. That's the real reason you are in the pit. He wants to bend you and shape you and form you through the heat of adversity. He wants to conform you to the image of Christ."[8]

The Bible is replete with people who find themselves beneficiaries- albeit unwillingly- of adversity. The opposition faced by Joseph at the hand of his brothers, David's mistreatment by Saul, and Elijah's difficulties with the wicked Ahab and Jezebel are but a few reminders of how God can stretch our faith in the face of adversity. God uses adversity in our lives to grow us and teach us. He uses our struggles to deepen our faith and strengthen our trust.

---

[8] Steve Farrar, Tempered Steel: How God Shapes a Man's Heart through Adversity (Sisters, OR: Multnomah Press, 2002), 32.

Romans 8:28 is a well known and exceptionally valuable verse. It teaches us that God can work in our lives for good despite the difficulties we face. "We know that all things work together for the good of those who love God," it says, "those who are called according to His purpose."

It is a great verse and a great promise. God will use the difficulties I face, even the adversity of life, for my good. My hurts will not be wasted. My problems will not be faced without an ultimate benefit.

The truth of this verse was poignantly taught me during a seminary class in Greek. Our professor brought us to Romans 8:28 and worked through the translation. Then, he talked to us about the meaning of the verse- not just the Greek to English meaning- the *meaning* of the verse.

Our professor, we knew, had lost his beloved wife in death just months earlier. He talked of the pain, the darkness and the struggles that accompanied such adversity. He also talked of the deep comfort that he ultimately found in knowing that God would use this terrible ordeal in ways that brought good.

Some, he said, had glibly quoted the verse to him in a well-meaning, but misguided attempt to bring him comfort. But Romans 8:28, he said, was not a verse to be quoted to others. It was a verse that one had to quote to one's self.

While knowing he would struggle with the pain of separation for the rest of his life, our professor also reminded us that he knew he would continue to experience the blessing of God's peace for the rest of his life. He knew that God would use the terrible adversity to bring important lessons, deepened understanding and long-term benefit.

That is a "Greek" lesson I will not soon forget. To see a man who had walked "through the valley of the shadow of death" and discovered God's presence and peace there was more valuable than any vocabulary lesson could ever be.

<u>Victors can face adversity</u>. Gideon was finishing the great victory over Midian when adversity came. (Judges 8:1ff.) Enemy forces had already lost 120,000 casualties. Only 15,000 enemy combatants and their two kings Zebah and Zalmunna were left. But the victors still faced some serious obstacles.

I remember years ago hearing a preacher named Ron Dunn say, "Victory and adversity often travel on parallel tracks and arrive about the same time." How often that has proven to be true. We might think that victory banishes our obstacles. But, in this world, in this life, obstacles have a way of popping up even on the heels of victory.

The first obstacle faced by Gideon and his men was exhaustion. Warfare can be hard work. Our church is near a large military facility and a number of military members and their families attend our fellowship. Many of them have been called to duty in hot, dusty, difficult parts of the world. They may serve in oppressive heat in some distant battlefield. Not only is the temperature excessive, but they labor under armored gear and heat-retaining helmets while lugging loads of equipment and weaponry.

Gideon's men were worn down from the rigors of the battlefield. Physical exertion, lack of sleep and the constant strain of dealing with the enemy left them drained and depleted. Judges 8:4 tells us "they were exhausted, but still in pursuit".

I'm sure many of you reading this have had moments like this. You are exhausted but there is still a job to do. The new mother is constantly busy (how many diapers can this child go through?) and never seems to be allowed to sleep through a night. But there is still a job to do. The laborer has worn himself out with work, but the job needs a little more effort. The office manager has already put in a full day, but there are still important tasks to finish.

Gideon's men were worn out. They just needed some rest and some assistance. But their fellow Israelites gave them neither.

A second obstacle Gideon and his army faced was doubt. Even their amazing victory of the past hours did not keep some from doubting their ability to finish the battle. The eighth chapter of Judges tells us that Gideon and his pursuers came to the town of Succoth- a town in Israel- and asked for bread for the weary soldiers pursuing the Midianite kings Zebah and Zalmunna.

It was a reasonable request. These kings had terrorized Israel for years. Now, Gideon's army had them on the run. They just needed some help. But the response of the men of Succoth drips with doubt. "Are Zebah and Zalmunna now in your hands that we should give bread to your army?" (Judges 8:6)

It didn't seem to matter that God had already routed most of the Midianite army. The cautious men of Succoth were taking no chance of being seen by Midian as aiding and abetting the rebellion. Succoth had lived under their domination enough to doubt things would ever change.

Parenthetically, Succoth wasn't the only group in Israel who had doubts about God's ability. Gideon might have forgotten that he sounded much like them- insecure and doubting- just days earlier when God first called him to leadership.

A third obstacle for Gideon was direct opposition. The leaders of the Israelite towns of Succoth and Penuel refused to help Gideon. They were unwilling to even give the soldiers who fought on their behalf the bread that would sustain them.

We might expect such opposition from our enemies. But Succoth and Penuel were towns in Israel. They were supposed to be on Gideon's side.

Opposition from friends and family is always the hardest to take. It is one thing for an outsider to oppose us, but entirely different to get no support from those who are supposed to be with us. To be doubted by outsiders is one thing. To be doubted by those who are closest to us is much more difficult to deal with.

Victors can lose perspective in the face of adversity. Gideon's lack of assistance from the Israelite towns of Succoth and Penuel teach us the answers to two important questions. Each of these questions deals with perspective.

The first question is "who do I trust"? Do I trust God or do I trust men? Do I depend upon Succoth and Penuel or is my faith in the Lord?

Adversity can cause us to think that we must depend upon people. If Succoth and Penuel don't come through we think we are in big trouble. The truth is that Succoth and Penuel- or people anywhere- are notoriously undependable.

Succoth and Penuel are undependable but the Lord is entirely dependable. You might not be able to trust people, but you can always trust God.

My young friend was deeply disappointed. He was a new Christian and had assumed everyone in Christian circles was trustworthy, reliable and sincere. But, as happens to everyone who meets enough of them, he had encountered some hypocritical church members. It shook him. It disillusioned him.

Not long after I had the opportunity to speak with this young man. He told me of his disappointment and I reminded him of two important principles. The first principle is that people will ultimately fail you. In some way, at some point, we are all less than our faith deserves. Even the best among us knows that we are "prone to wander" as the old hymn says. We can be blind to fault, unkind to others and less than pure in motives.

But I also reminded my friend that our trust is not in men- not in Succoth or Penuel or Sunday School teachers or pastors or mentors. Our faith is to be placed in the only one worthy of our trust- the Lord.

I would like to be a good example to others. I want to avoid the hypocrisy that so often stains the modern church. But I know that at my best I will still be imperfect. So I want to encourage people to place their faith in someone far more trustworthy than me. I want them to place their faith in the never-hypocritical, never-failing Lord.

The second question is "who is the enemy"? Was the enemy Succoth and Penuel? They had, after all, disappointed and failed Gideon and the army in their time of need. Losing perspective can cause us to see our brothers and sisters as the enemy. But we have an enemy far more dangerous than Succoth and Penuel.

A word needs to be said here. Our brothers and sisters in Christ are not the enemy. We can disagree with each other- even vigorously so. We can debate and discuss. If issues are grave enough we can even break fellowship. But our fellow believers are not the enemy.

The lost world is not the enemy. We disagree with the philosophies and dogmas of this world. We engage lost men and women in healthy debate and dialogue. We dislike wrong thinking and grieve over wrong actions. But the lost people themselves are not the enemy. "For our battle is not against flesh and blood, but against the rulers, against the authorities, against the world powers of this darkness, against the spiritual forces of evil in the heavens." (Ephesians 6:12)

<u>Victors can forget blessings in the face of adversity</u>. Despite the many blessings we receive it is easy to forget them when we face difficult times. Instead, we note our problems and focus solely upon them. After winning great victories, Gideon's focus is not on his blessings. His focus is squarely placed on those who have wronged him.

Israel wins the final victory in the war against Midian and her allies. You would think the immediate response of

Gideon and his men would be joy and thanksgiving to God. Instead, the first response is to seek revenge upon the leaders of Succoth who let the army of Gideon down. Judges 8:14 tells us that Gideon captures a young inhabitant of Succoth and forces him to write down the names of all the leaders of the city of Succoth. And he doesn't get the names in order to send them Christmas cards.

It is really hard to seek God and revenge simultaneously. One gets in the way of the other. When we seek God we have this tendency to love and to show grace. That messes up our plans for revenge. When we seek revenge we tend to forget God. We lose sight of his mercifulness on our behalf.

How many ways have you been blessed? In more ways than you can count? Yet, when we face adversity, we can find ourselves focused on our problems and forgetting our blessings.

Gideon wins such a great victory from God that you expect nothing but rejoicing and thankfulness for weeks. Instead, his focus after defeating Gideon seems to be only upon the way Succoth and Penuel had wronged him. It's funny (and not in the happy way) how we can forget our blessings when we face adversity.

Victors can lack mercy in the face of adversity. Mercy is an interesting concept. We seem to like receiving it more than giving it. Gideon was on the receiving end of much mercy from the Lord. God was patient with him when he doubted. God showed understanding to him when he lacked courage. But Gideon struggled to give mercy to the cities of Israel who had also doubted and lacked courage.

Jesus tells a great story about forgiveness in Matthew 18. There was a man who had a slave who owed him 10,000 talents. That is an impossible amount for any slave to ever hope of paying back. It is a crushing, hopeless debt. The master decided to sell the slave, his wife and his children in order to recoup what he could of the debt.

But on the way to the auction block an interesting thing occurs. The slave pleads for patience, even though the amount he owes can never be repaid. And, to the surprise of all who saw, the master decided to grant mercy. He forgave the loan. Mercy was received.

Sadly, the story doesn't end there. It turns out the slave is also owed some money. A fellow slave owes him the more manageable debt of 100 talents. It isn't 10,000 talents but it is still a sizable sum. You just know the story will end with the first slave showing the same mercy he received. But that is not what happened.

Receiving mercy is always easier than giving mercy. The first slave choked the second slave and demanded the money he was owed immediately. When the second slave couldn't pay he threw him into the debtor's prison. When the master finds out what has happened- well, let's just say it is an unhappy ending for the unforgiving slave.

We can be too much like that slave. We love receiving the mercy of God but struggle to give it to others. Gideon found God's mercy but was unwilling to bestow it on his fellow countrymen. In adversity we debtors can forget the forgiveness of debt God has granted to us.

Victors can teach failure in the face of adversity. The story of Gideon takes a rather sad turn in Judges 8:20-21. First, Gideon tells his son, still a youth, to kill the kings on his behalf. The boy is reluctant to do that. So, dad steps in and kills the kings himself. Then, dad teaches the boy a lesson that he will not easily forget. He teaches him that God gives victory so we can have some financial benefit. I'm not saying that is the lesson God wants taught. But it seems to be the lesson Gideon teaches nonetheless.

The Bible tells that Gideon kills the kings and then takes the crescent ornaments that were on the necks of the camels. These ornaments, especially for kings, were often elaborate and valuable. Made with gold and jewels, such an item could be very costly. And Gideon taught his son something-perhaps without ever realizing it.

Gideon's son learned something like this. "You lead so that you can get something. Be sure to get what you deserve. Take the best for yourself. Don't miss out on getting the finest things in life." That is the lesson Gideon seems to be teaching. It isn't the lesson God teaches, mind you, just the lesson that the son must have learned.

When we are selfish we teach others selfishness. When we are unforgiving we teach the same lesson to those who watch us. Failure, like victory, can be taught.

We are always teaching our children something. And we usually teach them more by what we do than by what we say. What lessons are your children learning?

Some of you are facing great adversity in your life right now. You didn't ask for it and you don't want or enjoy it. But I do want you to note that God stretches us through adversity. We can learn the lessons God wants to teach us through adversity if we will be open to them. God can use these events to open our eyes and our hearts to the important lessons of life.

Ask God to use this difficult season in a way that conforms you to the image of Christ. Ask the Lord to teach you new lessons and to give you a new understanding of trust. Allow the Lord to deepen your faith and strengthen your commitment to his perfect plan and purpose for your life.

Part Three: God Allows People to Make Surprising Choices

I'm often surprised by who makes it. We've all known some folks who seemed to have very limited talents and yet they were wildly successful in their occupation or their ministry or with their family. Or maybe they had the worst background, the most difficult family life, and the fewest advantages growing up. But they turned that difficult start into a spectacular finish.

I'm often surprised, as well, by who doesn't make it. They start with every advantage. They have doting parents, material wealth and the best educational opportunities. The sky is the limit for their potential. But they squander it all, waste their abilities and accomplish so little.

God allows some surprising choices. He allows those who have failed to choose to overcome. He allows the successful to choose to throw it all away.

I know a brother and sister who grew up in a dysfunctional home. The mother was gone and the father struggled with addiction. They spent much of their lives under the care of relatives. Interestingly, though they grew up in the same environment they each chose completely different paths. The sister became a committed follower of Christ. The brother was in constant trouble with the law and society. Both had similar backgrounds. Each made separate choices.

While the past affects you it doesn't have to define you. You can build on your past, learn from your past or be crushed by your past. But you can't blame your past for your future. You can and must make the choices which determine your direction. God allows you to choose which path you will follow. He allows us all to make surprising choices in life.

Chapter Ten: God Allows the Choice of Devotion

We all choose the object of our devotion. We can devote ourselves to work, to family, to hobbies or to folly. Our devotion can be to God or not. It can be partial or complete.

Devotion has to do with our love and commitment. It is about those things that most matter to us and fill our thoughts and dreams. It concerns the ultimate issues and guides our decisions and actions.

Gideon was faced with the choice of devotion. On the heels of great victory came important choices. Would his devotion to the Lord be long lasting or short term? Would he follow God in the hard times as well as the easy? Was his devotion limited to times of conflict or would it last beyond the battlefield? In considering your choice of devotion there are some things to remember.

With success comes temptation. Finally, we won! After a long series of close- and not so close- defeats, our First Baptist Academy basketball team broke through for a win. It was our first year fielding a team and we had faced many difficult losses. Our hard work seemed never to be rewarded. But finally a win came.

The danger that follows success is the temptation to relax. The hard work and diligent effort required to find success on the hard court can be replaced by relaxation and a lackadaisical attitude on the heels of victory.

In a similar way, those who have some spiritual success can be tempted to forget the attributes which led to the success. Deep faith can be replaced with expectations that things will always be as they are now. Deep devotion can be replaced with ritualistic activity. Where we once depended upon God, we can begin to depend upon ourselves.

I'm told that most of the accidents that occur among climbers of Mt. Everest happen on the way down rather than on the way up. Sometimes, the exhilaration of mountaintop success is followed by carelessness on the difficult descent.

I love the spiritual mountaintop. I love the joy of doing something big or important for God. But I need to remember to be faithful to God after the victory. The adversary is always willing to place a stumbling block in my way. The time after a victory can be a time when we are unprepared to face those stumbling blocks. We can forget, after the thrill of victory, the hard perseverance that is still required.

Trusting man instead of God. One potential stumbling block we can face after success is the temptation to trust ourselves instead of the Lord. Let me note three reasons you ought to trust God instead of trusting yourself. First, God is stronger than you are- even if you work out. Second, God is smarter than you are- even if you memorize the dictionary. Third, God is more dependable than you- even if you keep a "To Do List".

The Israelites were to trust God rather than man. After all, God is stronger, smarter and more dependable. But, immediately after God gave them victory over their enemy, they wanted to trust Gideon instead of the Lord. Judges 8:22 tells us that they asked Gideon and his sons and grandsons to rule over them. And the reason they gave was because "you (Gideon) delivered us from the power of Midian".

If ever there is a bible story that reminds us that the deliverance comes from God and not from man, the story of Gideon is it. God gave the victory, not Gideon or any man. God should be trusted, not people. Yet, something within Israel tempted them to place their faith in a man and his family rather than placing it in God and his purposes.

You, like Israel, will be tempted at times to trust yourself instead of God. Just ask yourself, when that temptation comes, "Am I stronger than God? Am I smarter than the Lord? Should I depend upon myself instead of the perfectly dependable Sovereign of the Universe?" I think the answer should be clear.

<u>Taking the glory which belongs to God</u>. Another temptation which the enemy places before us is the desire to take the credit and glory which rightly belongs to God. Gideon had it right when he said in Judges 8:23 "I will not rule over you, and my son will not rule over you; the Lord will rule over you." Gideon realized the important concept that God gave the victory and God deserved the glory.

Some of you reading this have been used by God to accomplish many great things. You have taught, preached, witnessed and led people to faith. There is a subtle danger that comes with that success. You may begin to think you deserve the glory which rightly belongs only to the Lord.

There is an old story about a preacher who preached to the best of his ability one Sunday morning. After the service, people lined up to shake the pastor's hand and provide words of encouragement. Being a humble man, the preacher wanted to respond in the proper way. So, when a little old lady thanked him for his sermon, the pastor responded by saying, "Don't thank me, thank God." She responded with, "It wasn't <u>that</u> good"!

Gideon, at least on this occasion, was able to realize that the victory belonged to the Lord. He was being praised, but the glory really belonged to God. "Don't thank me," he was saying, "thank God."

We must be very careful what we take credit for. There is really very little for which we should be praised. Should we take credit for our intellect, our talents, our strength or our calling? All these things are gifts provided by God. We can only take credit for having enough recognition of God's greatness and glory to use and sharpen those gifts. We can only get credit for having enough faith to believe God is able to use those gifts he has given us in a way that impacts our world. He deserves the glory- all of it. We should be thankful that God allows us to be part of the victories which he provides while never forgetting that he provides them.

Actions speak louder than words. What Gideon said did not match what he did. He said the glory belonged to the Lord. But the very next thing Gideon did was to ask everyone to give a golden earring from the plunder (Judges 8:24-27). The enemy wore gold in their ears and Gideon asked each man to give him one of those valuable trinkets. And Gideon did not want to collect those earrings for just any reason. He wanted to use them to make a golden ephod.

Gideon collected "about 43 pounds of gold" from the plunder. (Judges 8:26) That is a lot of gold. In the absence of banks, it was not uncommon for the people of that age to wear their wealth. The golden earrings they sported provided a safe way to keep track of their wealth. Any withdrawal is easy to track if the deposit is worn in your ear. So Gideon was able to make quite an ephod.

An ephod is a garment like a vest. It was worn by the priest in the temple. But it also had the danger of being used as an idol. So, let's get this straight. Gideon says with his lips, "We will only give glory to the Lord." But he says with his actions, "We are willing to compromise our worship of the

Lord by creating an idol just like the other countries." Which lesson do you believe was more memorable to the Israelites-the lesson of his words or the lesson of his actions?

Our actions are always more powerful than what we say. People are far more likely to remember how we act than how we speak. How you treat people will be remembered more clearly than what you say to them. Your behavior will last longer than your sermons.

We teach our children a great deal through our actions. A golfer was teaching some men the finer points of the game. He had his young son with him and decided to show the men what he had been teaching the lad. So he said to his son, "Son, show these men what I've taught you about playing golf." To his dismay, the young man reached down for the driver, screamed out a profanity and threw the golf club into the lake! The instruction of the golfer's life was far greater than his verbal instructions could ever be.

I want to remind my fellow pastors that the greatest messages we ever preach are the messages of our lives well lived. The greatest Sunday School lesson you will ever teach is the lesson of your life. The most influential part of your parenting is how you live in front of your children. These lessons may contradict our verbal instructions, but our actions will always outweigh our words in the long run.

<u>Blind spots</u>. One of the older ladies in my church struggles because she doesn't have peripheral vision. There is, in effect, a blind spot that keeps her from seeing things which are not directly in front of her. It causes problems for her with driving and other activities. Blind spots can be dangerous.

Perhaps the ephod was a blind spot for Gideon. Maybe he didn't make the connection between his commitment to worship only the Lord and his decision to build an ephod which could be used in idolatry. Is it possible that he had been so influenced by his culture that he was blind to the danger of idolatry?

Might we have some blind spots? Are there some areas where we have been so influenced by our culture that we cannot see the truth? There is always the possibility that we will miss those dangers which come wrapped as harmless decisions.

Often, people can easily see the problems in another person's life but struggle to see their own. They have great vision for the faults of others but have blind spots when it comes to their personal shortcomings. Many remain blissfully unaware of the problems, shortcomings and sins of their lives- seemingly oblivious to personal faults.

Wise are those who see the truth about themselves. Wise are they when they can recognize danger and see potential problems before they occur. And wise are those who keep their spiritual eyes open wide.

Repeating sins. Idolatry was a "repeating sin" in the life of Israel. Over and over the Bible tells of their return to this sinful activity. Maybe they returned to that sin because it was so common among the other nations. There is something in us that wants to be like the rest of the world. Or perhaps they returned to idolatry because it was easier than worshipping the Lord. Whatever the reason, Israel returned repeatedly to the worship of idols.

It did not take long for the Israelites to build the golden calf when Moses delayed in coming down from Mt. Sinai. Exodus 32 records the sad story of Israel's rapid abandonment of the Lord for a man-made calf of gold. They witnessed the Lord's miracles in bringing them from Egypt. But they were so prone to idolatry. They took their earrings off and gave them to Aaron who fashioned the calf into a golden idol. Then the people said that idol was the god who brought them out of Egypt. Idolatry was their repeating sin.

Are there any repeating sins in your life? Are there some points of weakness which you find yourself returning to frequently? Perhaps anger is a recurring attitude. Maybe pride easily slips into your heart. Possibly lust or coveting or jealousy ensnares your life easily.

One of the keys to dealing with these repeating sins is to acknowledge the problem. Recognize your tendency towards weakness in a particular area. And then, stay as far away from anything that leads to the problem as you can.

The alcoholic unwisely continues to frequent bars just for the food. He or she unwisely hangs out at parties where alcohol is consumed just to see friends. Instead, wisdom suggests that the alcoholic stays as far from the temptation and the danger as he or she possibly can.

In a similar way, you need to avoid those things which can cause you to stumble. Don't build an ephod to commemorate a victory. The danger is that ephod will soon turn to idolatry. Stay far from those activities or attitudes that have damaged your spiritual life in the past. Stop justifying, stop rationalizing and stay away as far from those things as possible.

Bad choices bring unintended consequences. Judges 8:27 says, "Gideon made an ephod from all this and put it in Ophrah, his hometown. Then all Israel prostituted themselves with it there, and it became a snare to Gideon and his household."

Did you notice that the ephod became a snare specifically to Gideon and to his household? It wasn't just a snare in general to Israel, it was a snare in specific to Gideon's own life and family.

I doubt that Gideon thought when he was collecting the gold and building the ephod, "You know, one day this will do great damage to my children and my grandchildren." I doubt he planned it that way. But there are always consequences to our choices. Some of those consequences were never intended but are painful nonetheless.

The choice Gideon made to build the ephod became a snare to him and to his family. The choices we make carry consequences as well. Often those consequences are felt most acutely by the people we love the most.

Fathers and mothers, I want you to do right because it is right. But please remember that your wrong choices don't affect just you. They also affect your children. You might not intend to harm them by your choices, but when you bring an ephod into your home, they will be affected whether you intended it or not.

Gideon built an ephod and all the Israelites prostituted themselves with it. An unwise choice led to unintended consequences. Israel was harmed by an unwise choice. Gideon's family was harmed by an unwise choice. And Gideon was harmed by his unwise choice.

Here is the good news. When we make wise choices others are blessed. When we make wise choices we are a blessing to our nation, our family and to ourselves. We should do right because it is right. But right brings consequences along with it. And the consequences of right choices are the blessings of God.

God allows the choice of devotion. On the heels of victory we can praise and glorify him or forget his blessings. We can turn to ourselves or we can remember his greatness and glory.

The choice of devotion is given to us all. We choose the object and intensity of our love and commitment. We choose what we give ourselves to and what we prioritize. We choose what matters most to us. I pray you will choose to give your devotion to the Lord. I pray you give it in full.

Chapter Eleven: God Allows People the Choice of Legacies

As I write this I'm grieving over the death of a friend. Just a few days ago, my friend and his son were killed in a terrible accident. I'm heartbroken for his family and his friends. I'm stunned by the suddenness of the loss. I'm saddened by the end of a life with such great potential for good. And, I'm reminded of the brevity and value of life.

I don't know if you've thought much about your own mortality. We don't need to be fixated on the subject, but perhaps it is good for us to consider some things about what we will leave behind when our life ends. What will people remember about us? What will our actions say about us? What lessons will we leave for future generations?

Our legacy includes the lessons we leave behind for future generations. For good or for bad we are choosing that legacy every day.

The story of Gideon ends with a focus on the legacy this "Warrior in Hiding" left behind. We see the good and the not so good. We see a little of the legacy he left to his children and the legacy he left to his nation. We see what was and we see what could have been.

My friend's death was unexpected. I'm sure he and his family anticipated many years of life ahead. But in the years

God gave him he left the legacy of a godly man, a godly family man and a godly servant of the Lord Jesus Christ. And that, my friends, is a great legacy to leave behind.

God teaches us some important legacy lessons through the life of Gideon. His legacy- both the positive and negative- teaches us lessons about what we leave behind.

God can use a warrior to bring freedom and peace. I live near Scott Air Force Base. There are many military families who live in our area and large numbers of the military community who attend our church. I often remind them that they have real job security.

The Bible tells us that there will be "wars and rumors of wars" (Mark 13:7) until the end of the age. That is, the condition of the human heart is such that there will always be sin and its consequences. There will always be sinful people trying to oppress others. There will be dictators and warlords and aggressors until the Lord returns. In other words, we will need the services of our military and police forces as long as there are sinful people living in this sinful world.

What would happen if we had no law enforcement in our land? Sinful people would still be involved in sinful acts. But, in the absence of people to inhibit sinful behavior, lawlessness would increase. Without the presence of lawmen, lawbreakers would have no check on their maliciousness. Sin would abound, society would be in danger of crumbling.

Law enforcement is designed to provide for peace. Military strength is, in its purest form, a means of keeping peace between nations.

In the days of the Wild West, the Colt Single Action Army handgun was know as the "Colt Peacemaker" because of its ability to keep crime from spreading. It was designed for the US government and stood as the standard handgun of military service. In more recent times, an Intercontinental Ballistic Missile carried the name "Peacekeeper". Built during the Cold War, the "Peacekeeper" was designed as a counterforce to Soviet nuclear threats. It would "keep the peace"- the concept went- by serving as a deterrent to Soviet aggression.

In the days of Gideon, peace was attained through the means of war. Judges 8:28 says, "So Midian was subdued before the Israelites, and they were no longer a threat." And the result of Gideon's battle becomes clear in the remainder of that verse. "The land was peaceful 40 years during the days of Gideon."

God used a warrior to bring freedom and lasting peace to Israel. It is a legacy lesson you should remember. God can bring freedom and lasting peace to people's lives through the battles that you fight under his command.

All believers are warriors. If you go way back in church life you might remember the song "I'm in the Lord's Army". It was a great song I often sang as a boy. The part I loved best was the motions which accompanied the singing. When we sang "I may never march in the infantry" we marched in place. When we sang "ride in the cavalry" we squatted and jumped up and down as though riding a war horse. When singing "shoot the artillery" we slapped our palms together simulating a burst of weaponry. And I'll never forget "zooming o'er the enemy" while turning my arms into the wings of a fighter jet doing combat with some aerial foe. I even got to salute at the part that said "But, I'm in the Lord's army".

We don't sing songs like that much anymore. Perhaps it is too hokey now, I'll grant you that. But maybe we don't sing about being in the Lord's army because we have forgotten that all believers are warriors.

Remember that God calls all believers into the spiritual battles of life. We have a cause, a daunting enemy and armor. We have the sword of God's word and the power of the Holy Spirit. And every believer is to be at his or her station.

Like Gideon, you may not realize that you are warrior material. If you are a believer, however, you have been drafted into service.

My father was drafted into the U.S. army twice. He reached the draft age just at the conclusion of the Second World War. When the war ended, he was discharged along with most of the soldiers.

When the Korean Conflict began, the draft was reinstituted. Those who had not served a full two years in the army were eligible to be drafted again. My father was one of the small group of soldiers who was drafted twice.

I was only drafted once and it wasn't for the U.S. army. I was drafted into the Lord's army the day I gave my life to Christ. I am a soldier- a warrior- in God's army. And so is every other believer in the Lord.

Warriors choose battles wisely. Soldiers don't have to do battle with every stray cat. (That's good because stray cats can be tough!) Being a warrior does not mean we fight everyone or everything at every time. We should choose our battles wisely.

My favorite analogy (well, I like the stray cat analogy as well) concerns the Lone Ranger. The Lone Ranger was a television show long years ago. He was a masked "good guy" in the old American West. He fought and defeated the hoodlums and criminals of his era.

The Lone Ranger had very unusual bullets. They weren't the normal bullets. They were bullets made of silver.

Now, if you have silver bullets you are careful with them. They are expensive. You don't shoot them off at just everything. They cost too much for that. You save those bullets for when you really need them.

That is how we are with battles. We don't just fight to fight. We should seek the battles the Lord has for us. We fight the battles he gives us to fight. Gideon had a battle with the Midianites. Maybe your battle is with the worldly mindset of some Junior High Sunday School students or with some injustice in society or with your own personal war against a hidden sin.

Warriors don't fight alone. Okay. I know it is increasingly popular to "church bash" but I want to say a good word about the church. Christ founded the church and he did it for a reason. And one really great reason is because we don't have to fight life's battles alone. We are a sort of spiritual band of brothers who get to serve in the Lord's army side by side.

Gideon only had 300 warriors alongside him. But he didn't have to fight alone. And even had God called him to do battle without any other man, the Lord would have been at his side every step of the way. The battle belongs to the Lord.

I've read many books on the history of American wars- from the pre-Revolutionary wars to the current conflicts facing American soldiers. It seems to me that one of the key ingredients to the success of the American military is the camaraderie and closeness of the soldiers. They become closer than brothers in those battlefield situations. They fight and serve for each other as well as for the cause.

We have the privilege of serving with other believers in our spiritual battles. And we need each other. We need to work together, serve together and sacrifice together. We will face battles in this life, but we don't have to face them alone.

God can accomplish great things through surprising people. Another legacy lesson we learn from Gideon is that God accomplishes great things through surprising people. Gideon was such an unexpected choice to lead the nation of Israel out of bondage. But God saw the warrior in hiding and God used him despite how average, how ordinary he appeared to others.

Others may be surprised that God would choose us to do anything great. But God sees in us what others cannot see. He sees the warrior in us, even when that warrior hides and shirks responsibility and lives in fear instead of victory.

I sometimes think God enjoys surprising us with the people he chooses. Who would guess the shepherd boy David would lead the nation? Who would have picked the persecutor Saul to instruct the church? Maybe you aren't on the top of the "A" list, but God wants to use you as well.

God does extraordinary things through ordinary people. I don't have a giant letter S on my t-shirt. (I just checked; it isn't there.) I don't have a famous lineage. (I can't seem to find the Earl of Munton in my family tree.) I don't even really have any spectacular talents. (I don't think my ability to spit can be classified as a "spectacular talent" but I could be wrong.) I'm kind of an ordinary person. But the good news is that God does extraordinary things through ordinary people.

Charles Stanley is famous in Evangelical circles. He has been a pastor in Atlanta for many years and his messages are broadcast on television and radio all over the world. I was in the African country of Uganda, of all places, and there was Charles Stanley on their television. Unfortunately, the television moved from Dr. Stanley's message directly into a Madonna video without even a commercial break. But, none-theless, Charles Stanley's preaching was broadcast even on another continent.

I got to meet Dr. Stanley not long ago. You know what struck me about him? He was a normal man. No super powers that I could tell. No leaping of tall buildings. But God has used him in amazing ways to proclaim the message of Christ.

Have you ever considered that your "ordinariness" is something that God can use? Perhaps some listen to you talk of your relationship with God because they can relate to you.

You have some of the same tendencies and background and personality issues that they have. And God uses you.

God wants to accomplish great things through your life. Being ordinary has not fooled God. He knows you can accomplish great things with your life through him. He sees the warrior in you even when you are hiding behind the excuse of your weakness.

An older lady in our church had physical problems which kept her from doing the things she used to do in our church. She could no longer sing in the choir or teach the children's Sunday School class. She sighed and lamented to me, "Now, all I can do for the church is pray."

All she can do is pray? But didn't she realize that prayer is right at the front lines of the battle? Didn't she see the greatness of that activity? All you can do is use your ordinary life to accomplish the extraordinary purposes which God has for you. All you can do is use your limited abilities to accomplish God's incredible plans for you. All you can do is participate in the fabulous work of a fathomless God using your ordinary self. That's all.

One can lead a nation and lose a family. Here is where the Gideon story turns really sad. Gideon led the nation but he lost his family. It is a legacy lesson of which we all need to be aware.

Gideon was not a "one woman man". The Bible tells us that he had many wives. Gen. 2:24 says, "That is why a man leaves his father and mother and bonds with his wife, and they become one flesh." Like many of his time, Gideon lost sight of God's original purpose and plan for monogamous marriage. He used his wealth and influence to obtain many wives. These wives bore Gideon 70 sons. It was quite a family.

But the family doesn't stop there. Gideon had a concubine. She did not have the benefits of marriage, but Gideon was intimate with her as well. And from that inappropriate relationship came a son. His name was Abimelech.

Abimelech and his mother did not live with the rest of Gideon's family. They lived in Shechem. Abimelech's mother was a concubine, not a wife.

Abimelech and his mother weren't invited, I suspect, to the Thanksgiving turkey carvings or New Year's Eve get-togethers with the rest of the Gideon family. Abimelech didn't play catch in the back yard with his father. Dad didn't come to the parent-teacher conferences.

Abimelech must have grown up with some resentment and some ambition. Because, when Gideon died, Abimelech murdered the rest of the brothers with the exception of one who escaped. And, for a time, he became the ruler of the region.

My daughters both married recently. It is a strange time in a man's life when his daughters marry. They are no longer his little girls. They leave him, move in with some hairy legged boy and life changes. It is a time of reflection.

When your daughters marry, you don't regret the time you spent with them. You think back with joy to the silly songs and family games. You remember the vacations and events and time spent together.

Abimelech didn't have those memories. What he had was an absentee father- a father who never bothered to marry his mother. Abimelech must have grown up looking for the affirmation of a father, the example of a father, the love of a father. He got none of these things.

Many of you reading these words are parents. I hope you do well in your career goals. I pray you are a good neighbor and friend. But I plead with you to remember your responsibilities as a father or mother.

Leave a legacy of love and instruction to your children. Give them something more than your DNA. Give them you.

Compromised faith leads to collapsed faith. This is a legacy lesson of great importance. The compromises of one generation often lead to the collapses of another.

We are told in Judges 8:33-35 that after Gideon died, the Israelites turned from worship of God to idolatry. They became Baal worshippers just like their neighbors. They forgot God who had delivered them from their enemies. And they forgot the blessings God brought to them through the life of Gideon.

Israel fell back into the old familiar pattern. They disobeyed God, God judged them, they repented, God forgave and delivered them. Now, after God's deliverance, Israel went right back into idolatry and disobedience.

Once you open the crack of compromise, the chasm of collapse is nearby. There is a close connection between verse 27 and verse 33 in Judges 8. Verse 27 tells us of the compromise of a golden ephod that became a snare to Gideon and his household. Verse 33 tells us of the collapse of the next generation into full blown Baal worship.

Every church is a generation from apostasy. All who are familiar with the faith know of churches which were once vibrant and alive for Christ which are now barely attended and facing closure. We know of denominations which once burned passionately for the Lord but now are little more than religious social clubs who have lost sight of the gospel message.

Our building codes pay strict attention to compromise. The materials used in buildings must be sound. There can be no flaws in the steel or cracks in the foundation. Builders know that compromised materials can lead to collapsed structures. They build accordingly.

Pay attention to the compromises you allow into your life. Without holiness and repentance, the foundation of your life will be weak. And weak foundations inevitably lead to fallen structures.

Like Gideon we will all leave legacies of some sort. What are you leaving behind for your family and your circle of influence? What lessons do they take from the way you've lived the life God has given to you?

Conclusion

Few Bible characters are as interesting as Gideon, the warrior in hiding. Perhaps it is because we can see so much of ourselves in his doubts and insecurities. Maybe we are intrigued by the surprising way God uses this surprising man.

Whether we are hiding in our own wine vat, doubting and questioning God with our own fleeces or leading a charge against seemingly insurmountable odds, we can all relate to him. We can see a little of our own lives in his life. The lessons of his life still speak to us today.

Maybe you are a warrior in hiding. You doubt and fear. But God sees so much potential in you. He sees what you can be. He sees the warrior he knows you can be.

Listen, the kingdom of God needs some warriors today. We need some men and women who step out of the wine vat and onto the battle field. We need some men and women who fear only God and attempt great things for his glory. We need some who will trust God more than they fear the world.

God sees you there, hiding in the background. He sees your doubt and your tentativeness. But he also sees the gleam in your eyes that longs for something greater than your wheat threshing. He sees the warrior in you and invites you to participate in this great journey of faith that is lived out on the battlefield of life.

Printed in the United States
126427LV00002BA/2/P

9 781606 476475